Vern Per____
Rt. 3, Box 104-J Sp. 16
Brookings, Oregon 97415
Feb. 15, 1980

THIS WAS
RAILROADING

THIS WAS RAILROADING

by

GEORGE B. ABDILL

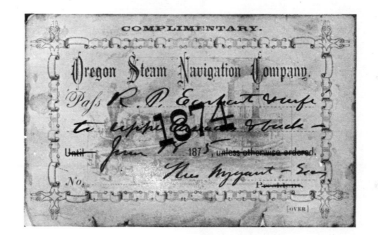

BONANZA BOOKS · NEW YORK

TWIN RIBBONS OF SILVER, THE STEEL TRAIL
CURVES AROUND THE BEND ON THE MAIN LINE
OF MEMORIES TO THE YEARS WHEN THE PACIFIC
NORTHWEST AND ITS RAILROADS WERE YOUNG
TOGETHER.

Dedication

For
Annette, Mike
and
my parents

NORTHERN PACIFIC RAILROAD

THOMAS F. OAKES, HENRY C. PAYNE, HENRY C. ROUSE,   RECEIVERS.

Pass   A. McDonald ------

Asst. G. F. & P. A. Man. & N. W. Ry

UNTIL DECEMBER 31ST 1895 UNLESS OTHERWISE ORDERED.

№ 1029   J. W. Kendrick
                              GENERAL MANAGER.

NOT GOOD UNLESS COUNTERSIGNED BY F. J. SHEPARD

T. E. HOGG., RECEIVER

Oregon Pacific Railroad Co.

RAIL AND RIVER DIVISIONS.

Pass Hon. R. P. Earhart & Wife

Complimentary

UNTIL DECEMBER 31 UNLESS REVOKED.

NOT GOOD UNLESS COUNTERSIGNED BY WM HOAG.

№ 230   T. E. Hogg
                        RECEIVER.

FOREWORD

This book is the outgrowth of an avocation that the writer has followed avidly for nearly twenty years. The fascination of the steam locomotive led to a career in engine service and a hobby of collecting photographs and data on the Iron Horse in the Northwest.

The quest has been a pleasant one, and has resulted in the development of a healthy respect for the veteran railroaders who carried on under conditions that now seem nearly impossible. These old-timers did their job and passed on, leaving no markers to honor their remarkable role in the opening of our sprawling region. Let this be a tribute to the courage and devotion to duty to those who pioneered on our steel trails.

Stories of our Northwest railroads would fill volumes and the limited space permitted only a skimming of the surface. Effort has been made to select photographs that depict the human side of railroading during the era of steam. The text has been checked for accuracy, although much of the history lies buried in dusty files and has grown exceedingly dim with the swift passage of the years. To present some idea of the task of compiling and editing the data, let it be known that there were thirty-six different railroads in operation or about to start construction in Washington alone in the year 1889. It has not been practical to mention every road, but the ones chosen are representative of the various major and short-line pikes that operated on the Pacific Slope.

The kindness of railroading friends and farflung corporations alike has aided immensely in assembling the material. The writer is grateful to all who have helped, including Guy Dunscomb, Modesto, California; E. D. Culp, Salem, Oregon; Miss Priscilla Knuth, Research Associate, Oregon Historical Society, Portland, Oregon; Willard E. Ireland, Provincial Archivist, Victoria, British Columbia; Miss Virginia Walton, Historical Society of Montana, Helena, Montana; Professor Charles J. Keim, Director of Information, University of Alaska; Martin Schmitt, Oregon Collection, University of Oregon, Eugene, Oregon; Jim Hartley, Simpson Logging Company, Shelton, Washington; Ross Youngblood, Bureau of Land Management, Coos Bay, Oregon; J. E. Broyles, Moscow, Idaho; Jack Slattery, Jack's Photo Shop, and "Curly" Richardson, Coos Bay, Oregon; Clement Wilkins, Coeur d'Alene, Idaho; Frank Herzog, Curator, Siskiyou County Historical Society, Yreka, California; Ralph Wortman, McMinnville, Oregon; Ernie Plant, Horseshoe Bay, British Columbia, and a host of generous railroad men who have dug into dust-covered trunks to unearth and donate photographs of the good old days.

Special thanks are due to Mr. Fred Jukes, veteran master rail photographer of Blaine, Washington, and Mr. H. H. Arey, of the Northern Pacific Terminal Company, Portland, Oregon. Mr. Jukes has been turning out engine photos of unexcelled quality since the 1890's. Mr. Arey, a rail photographer in his own right, has the fine collection of his father, the late H. L. Arey, for many years a locomotive engineer in Western Oregon.

Invaluable assistance was generously given by the Northern Pacific Railway, Union Pacific Railroad, White Pass & Yukon Route, Canadian Pacific Railway, Southern Pacific Company, Pacific Great Eastern Railway, Yreka Western Railroad, Great Northern Railway, Canadian National Railways and the Chicago, Milwaukee, St. Paul & Pacific Railroad.

The pleasurable chore of assembling the book could scarcely have been accomplished without the patience and sympathetic understanding of my wife, who lent her moral support and kept the coffee pot steaming.

This Was Railroading

Railroading is more than just a job . . . it is an undefinable substance that attaches itself to a man in so strong a manner that he is scarcely ever able to free himself from its grasp. It is a dog's life and men curse it, for it tears them from their homes and loved ones, demanding service in the black of the night when most civilized people are snugly abed. It is nerve-racking and exacting . . . not a man in train service that has not known fear when a foot stumbles or a mitt slips on a grab-iron while the rolling wheels grind underfoot; enginemen know the clutch at the heart when the monster machine they command bears down upon the heedless or unwitting.

Yet railroading is more than this . . . it is not all sorrow nor danger nor the sweat generated in broiling cabs on sultry summer days. It is the subtle combination of many ingredients . . . the odor of steam and hot valve oil mingled with the perfume of spring, newly-plowed earth, the scent of lilacs. It is the glory of sunrise bursting over the heights of the Cascades, the warm bath of the harvest moon over valley farmlands. It is wild geese circling over the green spring grain, and the cock pheasant crowing in the yellow stubble, the antlered buck that lifts a dripping muzzle from the trackside creek.

Railroading is the beat of driving rain and the numb chill of wading through hip-deep snow; the red glow of caboose stoves when the wind howls around the cupola and the air in the "crummy" is thick with the aroma of strong coffee brewing over a coal fire, blue with tobacco smoke and the fumes of oil lamps. It is the throb of air pumps, the pounding of rain on the storm windows, the chorus of frogs in the ditches at blind sidings. It is the roar of blasting exhausts and pounding rods as a "drag" thunders past, the clickety-clack of rail joints beneath the caboose, the drumming of drivers crossing trestles.

Railroading is the bright streak of color that marks the flight of the streamliner, the solitary glow of the green eye of a block signal, the swath a headlight cuts into the night, pointing out the towering shape of the firs . . . it is the clang and rattle of tank spouts when heat waves dance over the shimmering rails and the odor of creosote wafts across the cool patch of shade cast by dripping water tanks.

Blend with these ingredients the flickering glow of a torch as some "runner" oils around, the smoke plume that trails the local freight, the warm lights shining from farmhouse windows. Add the clash of drawbars and the rattle of slack, the staccato bark of the "goat" when the yard crews are sorting cars, and the squeal of flanges on steel rails.

Stir in a breath of the desert sage, the haunting reek of tidelands, and the glorious riot of color as the sun sinks into the western sea and the pungent aroma of woodsmoke drifts in a haze through the evergreens of the coastal hills.

A dash of the romantic names of far-flung places . . . Kamloops, Bonner's Ferry, Tenino, Revelstoke, Umatilla, Dunsmuir, Quesnel and Rathdrum . . . the chatter of sounders as the telegraph speaks across the miles.

Mix these with the ribald joke and hearty laughter, the hand lifted in comradeship as crews meet, the gentle deeds covered with a gruff mantle to hide the tenderness, and you will have the essence of that mystic compound called railroading.

TABLE OF CONTENTS

TABLE OF CONTENTS

LOWER CASCADES TERMINAL of the Cascade Railroad Co. was on Washington side of Columbia River. This view, taken about 1862-63, shows the engine house, turntable, and one of first portage engines at left; more modern locomotive in foreground is the **"D. F. BRADFORD."** Unidentified engine with coach, partly obscured by smoke, stands before building that housed coaches and railroad office. (Courtesy of Union Pacific R.R.)

The Columbia Gorge

THE PORTAGE ROADS

The colorful portage railroads that operated at the Cascades had their beginning in 1851 when F. A. Chenoweth built a wooden tram road on the north bank of the Columbia River. Cars ran from the steamboat landings, portaging both freight and passengers around the rocky reefs that studded the river. The motive power on the Chenoweth road consisted of mules, used to pull cars over the wooden rails.

Chenoweth sold this portage road to Daniel T. and Putnam F. Bradford and the line was renovated and extended to the lower Cascade landing. The repair work was under way in 1856 when the Yakima Indians swooped down on the Cascades settlements in March, the attack beginning on the 26th at about 8:30 A.M. A number of bridge carpenters were at work on the railroad bridges when the Indians first attacked, and one was killed and several wounded. These men ran down the track until they overtook some of the mule-drawn tram cars; the mules were cut loose and the carpenters and drivers made for the block house at the Middle Cascades. The Indians were out in force near a spring near the tracks and from there on to the block house the fleeing men ran a gauntlet of arrows and rifle fire, one of them being killed in the retreat. The Indians were later driven off by soldiers led by Lt. Phil Sheridan, and once again the portage road resumed operations. The Bradford road enjoyed a monopoly on the tremendous portage business at the Cascades and in 1858 an opposition line was started on the south bank of the river by J. O. VanBergen, who soon sold his road to J. S. Ruckle and H. Olmstead. They obtained the services of J. W. Brazee, a civil engineer, and pushed the road to completion in 1861. The Bradfords had incorporated their north bank tramway as the Cascades Railroad, so Ruckle & Olmstead named their south bank line the Oregon Portage Railway.

The flood of 1861 sent the Cascades Railroad under water, but the Oregon Portage Railway was able to maintain service.

The Oregon Steam Navigation Company obtained control of both these portage roads, but allowed the road on the Oregon side to fall into ruin, continuing to operate the Cascades R.R. on the Washington shore.

RAILROADING AND LUMBERING have gone hand in hand in the Northwest since pioneer times. View shows mule-drawn car on portage railway at the Cascades and water-power sawmill at left, probably in the late 1850's.

OUT OF THE DIM PAST rolls the beginning of railroad transportation in the Oregon Country. A long-eared mule was the motive power used to draw this car over the wooden stringers faced with strap-iron on the Portage railroad at the Cascades; similar line was built around the falls of the Willamette at Oregon City. Tepee-shaped tent at right was portable dark-room used to develop photographer's glass plates on the spot, a necessity of the 1850's when this view was taken. (Courtesy of Union Pacific R.R.)

The Oregon Portage Railway, however, laid claim to the first steam locomotive in the Northwest. This was the tiny 0-4-0 engine called the "Oregon Pony." She was built by the Vulcan Iron Works of San Francisco and shipped up to the Cascades where she made her initial trip on the morning of May 10, 1862. Engineer Theodore A. Goffe had put the "Pony" into running order and was at the throttle on her maiden trip. This little steamer was built for 5-foot

"D. F. BRADFORD," named for pioneer portage railroad operator, ran on Oregon Steam Navigation portage line between The Dalles and Celilo. Engine was uncommon 4-2-4 type, with only a single pair of driving wheels.

gauge track, and was later shipped back to California; still later, she was returned to Oregon and presented as a gift to the people of the state, now being on permanent display in the plaza fronting the Portland Union Station.

The canopy that now covers her boiler-head and tank were not originally a part of her equipment, and on her maiden trip she sloshed some boiler water over into her tiny cylinders. This was thrown out the smokestack by the exhaust, mixed with soot and cinders. The deluge of greasy water fell on a number of dignitaries who had climbed aboard for the first run; among the drenched spectators were Col. J. S. Ruckle, owner of the pike, and financiers W. S. Ladd, S. G. Reed and R. R. Thompson.

The Cascade Railroad was rebuilt after the flood of 1861, and the Oregon Steam Navigation Co. also constructed another portage railroad extending from The Dalles to Celilo. Both of these new lines used regular T-shaped iron rail instead of the wooden stringers faced with strap iron previously used at the Cascades. The Cascades and the Celilo roads both began their operations on April 20, 1863, each using a single crude steam locomotive. These two engines were named "ANN" and "BETSY," and one, or possibly both, of them were obtained by Ben Holladay for construction of the Oregon Central Railroad south from Portland. After a short time, more conventional locomotives were placed in service on both segments of the portage lines.

OREGON PONY was first locomotive in Pacific Northwest. Built by the Vulcan Iron Wks., San Francisco, she ran on Oregon Portage Ry. at the Cascades in 1862. (Photo Oregon Collection, University of Oregon)

The Cascade Railroad was the scene of the first fatal rail accident in the Northwest. At both ends of the line were inclines leading down to the wharf boats, and it was the practice to let the freight cars roll down these grades by gravity, controlled by a brakeman who manned the hand brake on the car. One day an Indian woman with a baby stepped out onto the incline, unnoticed by the crew. She failed to hear the silently-rolling car and was struck by it, the baby being killed.

In 1880 the Cascade Railroad was renovated and the original broad-gauge tracks, 5 feet wide, were changed over to the standard gauge of four feet, eight and one-half inches.

A short time later, the gauge was again changed, this time being reduced to three feet, or narrow gauge. This last change was to permit the use of the equipment of the Walla Walla & Columbia River Railroad. Henry Villard had acquired the old Oregon Steam Navigation Company and used it as the nucleus of his Oregon Railway & Navigation Company, and had acquired the Cascade Railroad in the deal. When the O.R.&N. took over the Walla Walla & Columbia River Railroad, the six little narrow-gauge engines belonging to the line were dis-

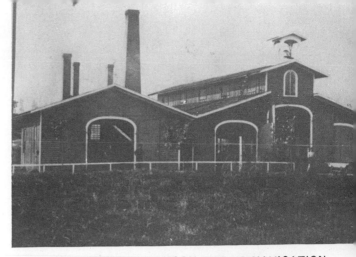

RAILROAD SHOPS OF OREGON STEAM NAVIGATION CO. were housed at these structures in The Dalles in the 1860's. Built in 1863, the first shop force here consisted of a foreman, three machinists, a boilermaker and a blacksmith. (Courtesy of Union Pacific R.R.)

posed of to various concerns; the W.W.&C.R. Engine No. 3, named the "COLUMBIA," was an 0-6-0 type built by Porter, Bell & Co. in 1876, and she became the Cascade Railroad No. 1.

Walla Walla & Columbia River Engine No. 4, the "BLUE MOUNTAIN," was a 2-6-0 (Mogul) type, and was also a Porter, Bell & Co. product, having been out-shopped in 1878. She became the Cascade Railroad No. 2.

PRIMITIVE LOCOMOTIVE used on the Cascade Rail Road, portaging freight and passengers around the Cascades of the Columbia River. Engine was placed in service in the early 1860's. (Courtesy of Oregon Historical Society)

When the main line of the O.R.&N. was completed between Portland and The Dalles, there was but little work left for the Cascade Railroad, portaging the freight of the independent boat lines operating on the Columbia. The high water of 1894 played havoc with the upper end of the line and the O.R.&N. leased the remaining lower portion to a salmon packing concern who used it to haul boxes of fresh fish from their fish wheels to the steamer connection at the lower landing. Eventually even this service was discontinued and the road fell into disrepair.

However, the end of the line was not yet in sight. In 1906 Jim Hill's Spokane, Portland & Seattle, the "North Bank Road," was being projected along the Columbia and it sought to condemn a right of way that crossed the old Cascade R.R. in no less than four places.

The Harriman interests, controlling the Union Pacific, suddenly recalled that they still owned the Cascade portage, having acquired it along with the O.R.&N. properties. In a last-ditch effort to keep the Hill lines out of their region, they fought the proposed condemnation clear to the United States Supreme Court, but lost out on the decision. Hill was allowed to build his North Bank Road, but was made to rebuild and relocate the Cascade Railroad, so that the new line only crossed it twice. Business dwindled to nothing and the Union Pacific allowed the old pike to die.

The portage road between The Dalles and Celilo came to a better end. The Oregon Railway & Navigation Co. acquired it from the O.S.N. and it became a part of Villard's line east to connect with the Northern Pacific and the Oregon Short Line.

In October, 1880, the President of the United States, Rutherford B. Hayes, passed over the line on his way to Walla Walla. In the party were Mrs. Hayes, Secretary Ramsey, and General William T. Sherman, of Civil War fame.

The Celilo portage road played a minor role in the Bannock Indian War of 1878. Indians were reported lurking along the line and troops brought up from Fort Vancouver, but before they arrived, a party of volunteers from the terminal at The Dalles mounted the train and sallied forth to do battle with any hostiles found along the tracks between there and Celilo

FOUR CARS was big load for this single-driver Danforth, Cooke & Co. locomotive of Oregon Steam Navigation shown here in service on the portage railroad along Columbia River between The Dalles and Celilo.

The train was in charge of Engineer Johnny Carey and Conductor Neal McFarland, and though a careful watch was kept, no hostiles were discovered.

In later years, two other portage lines were built on the Oregon side of the Columbia River. In September, 1891, the Oregon Portage Railway was placed in operation on the south bank at the Cascades, sponsored by the Oregon State Board of Portage Commissioners. This line hoped to break the monopoly of the O.R.&N. but it was short-lived. Part of the track had to be relocated to permit construction of the Cascade Locks, and the lower incline washed away in the flood of 1894, causing delay and more reconstruction. The road was discontinued in May of 1896, when the Cascade Locks were opened for use.

The other portage road of later days was the Oregon State Portage Railroad; this line was also built with State funds and ran from Big Eddy, four miles east of The Dalles, to a terminus at Celilo, following the old O.S.N. portage route. This new road was completed in September of 1905, but the Union Pacific promptly cut its rate on wheat and most of the grain trade moved by rail. In an effort to encourage traffic, the Legislature appropriated money to extend the line from Big Eddy into The Dalles and this was done, but the opening of the Celilo Canal removed any excuse for the existence of the Oregon State Portage Railroad and it was abandoned in 1915.

On the Washington side of the Columbia Paul Mohr had projected a portage railway around Celilo, but this venture went broke and was sold at a sheriff's sale held at Goldendale, Washington, on May 24, 1902.

Thus ends the saga of the portage railroads along the lower reaches of the Columbia River. They served in a very colorful era and were important pawns in the game for control of transportation through the Columbia George. Many famous steamboats discharged freight and passengers at their wharf boats and landings. A motley crowd of humans passed over their short reaches of trackage; settlers, miners, soldiers, gamblers, men and women of high station and low, all jostled over the rough tracks that flanked the mighty River of the West.

Today the long Diesel-powered freights and sleek streamliners roar over the transcontinental lines that thread through the Gorge and the noise of their passing must be sweet music to the bones of the slumbering railroaders who met death on the old portage road at the hands of the Indians on that bloody morning over one hundred years ago.

PIONEER GATEWAY
(Oregon Railway & Navigation Co.)

The historic railroad along the south bank of the Columbia River had it's start in 1879 when Henry Villard organized the Oregon Railway & Navigation Company. This concern included the portage railways at the Cascades and Celilo, the river boats of the Oregon Steam Navigation Company, the ocean interests of the Oregon Steamship Company, and the Walla Walla & Columbia River Railroad.

Villard desired to form a connection with a transcontinental line, using his Columbia River route as a vital link, and he offered the Union Pacific an opportunity to utilize his project. They declined, and in 1880 an agreement was completed with the Northern Pacific. Villard was to construct a railroad between Portland and a junction with the Northern Pacific at Wallula, giving the N.P. a direct connection to a Pacific Coast port.

"S. G. REED" was early wood-burner operated by Oregon Steam Navigation Co. in the 1870's, later became O.R.&N. Co.'s No. 4. Note the elaborate headlight bracket and fancy brass scroll plate between driving wheels which bore names of builders, Danforth, Cooke & Co.

"J. S. RUCKEL" was a pioneer locomotive operated by Oregon Steam Navigation Co. on portage railroad at the Cascades. Engine was built by Danforth, Cooke & Co. at Patterson, New Jersey, and later became Ore. Ry & Nav. Co. No. 3.

OLD BLOCKHOUSE AT UPPER CASCADES, (far left in above photo) looks down on portage railroad and settlement, scene of Indian attack in the Yakima War of 1856. Steamboat "ONEONTA" lies at wharf boat at far right; mixed train, consisting of two coaches, two box cars, and one flat car loaded with a covered wagon, is coupled behind O.S.N. locomotive. Screen for arresting sparks can be seen in top of engine's funnel smoke stack.

Work was begun early in 1880, under Superintendent of Construction John L. Hallett, along a line laid out by Chief Engineer Hans Thielsen. Construction of bridges was supervised by A. J. McLellan. Gangs of graders started east from Celilo and west from Wallula, and 7,500 tons

of rails were ordered from Cardiff, Wales. By May of 1880 the grade from Celilo was 7 miles east of the mouth of the John Day River and by October the line from Wallula had entered Umatilla. On the evening of April 16, 1881, the first through train chuffed out of The Dalles

also pushed along, the first train arriving at the Cascades on March 17, 1882. The entire road between Portland and The Dalles was completed on October 3, 1882, but the first train over the line was not run until November 21st of that year.

In addition to the foregoing main line construction, a branch was started east from Umatilla and completed to Pendleton on September 11, 1882.

The crowning event in the saga of the Oregon Railway & Navigation Company came in August and September of 1883. On August 25th the first through shipment of freight left Portland for St. Paul, Minnesota, and the first through passenger trains arrived, after the N.P. spike ceremonies, on September 10-11, 1883.

The rugged nature of the region traversed by the O.R.&N. presented many obstacles to railroad operation. East of The Dalles, the shifting sand dunes often buried the track. In 1882 such a sand drift near Alkali, 54 miles east of The Dalles, blockaded the tracks to a depth of 6 to 8 feet. Snow plagued the line in winter and floods often damaged the road. A flood in December of 1882 marooned a passenger train on the Baker City branch between Echo and Pendleton and carried away the bridge at Umatilla.

Another thorn in the side of the maintenance and operating departments was the "Sliding Mountain," located in the Columbia Gorge one mile west of the Cascades. A great natural fault there extended from 6 to 7 miles back into the mountain, and the face confronting the railroad was over a mile long. In the winter of 1894 this giant slide oozed out over 40 feet, pushing the tracks into the Columbia River. It was necessary to keep a gang of workmen there constantly, digging away the muck and rocks.

PORTAGE ROAD POWER. The J. C. AINSWORTH served on the Oregon Steam Navigation line between The Dalles and Celilo in the 1860's. (Courtesy of John T. Labbe and D. L. Stearns)

at 6:00 P.M., bound for Wallula.

Upon arrival at Wallula, the passengers were transferred to the narrow-gauge cars of the Walla Walla & Columbia River Railroad for the journey on the Walla Walla. This section was later converted to standard gauge, the change beginning in 1882.

Work on the road west from The Dalles was

FOGGING HER UP, the fireman of O.R.&N. Co.'s 84 shakes the grates to make a smoke cloud for the photographer near Hood River. Picture was probably made in the late 1880's. (Courtesy of John T. Labbe)

Large numbers of Chinese were employed in construction of the road and were frequently involved in accidents. In February of 1883, a gang of the Orientals were working near Portland when one of the crew chopped into a keg of black powder with an axe. The resulting explosion sent 10 of the Chinamen to join their illustrious ancestors.

Extensive shops and terminals for the road were maintained at Albina, a suburb of Portland, and at The Dalles. The shops at The Dalles were on a peninsula jutting out into the Columbia, and were originally started by the Oregon Steam Navigation Co. in 1863. John Torrence was the first foreman there, with Machinists Thomas Smith, James M. Smith, and John Wait, Blacksmith William Harman, and Boilermaker William Marshall. In 1866, J. M. Smith succeeded Torrence as foreman and held the job until 1877, when J. F. Curtis was ap-

pointed Master Mechanic. Curtis was replaced in 1882 by C. C. Hobart. By 1889, the O.R.&N. had a substantial roundhouse, tin shop, car shop, casting shop, carpenter shop, and blacksmith shop in operation there, plus offices, drafting room, and numerous storage sheds and tanks.

In later years, the repair facilities were shifted to Albina, the western terminus of the road.

Sponsored by the Union Pacific, the new Oregon Short Line thrust a line toward the Northwest in 1882. The O.S.L. left the parent road at Granger, Wyoming, and reached the Idaho border in June of 1882. The O.R.&N. extended its branch from Pendleton into the Blue

SNAKE RIVER CROSSING. Desolate hills form backdrop for early train of the Oregon Short Line in this photo taken in the 1880's. Bridge piers are hand-dressed stone. (Courtesy Oregon Historical Society)

WORK TRAIN pauses on Sandy River bridge near Troutdale, Oregon, in autumn of 1882. Locomotive is O.R.&N. No. 11, Baldwin-built Mogul type which later became the Tacoma Eastern R.R. No. 1. Wooden truss bridge was common type of structure on Northwest railroads for many years. (Davidson photo)

Mountains to meet the Oregon Short Line. The O.R.&N. tracks reached La Grande in June, 1884, and arrived in Baker on September 6th, being completed into Huntington on November 11, 1884. Here the two roads met, and on January 1, 1885, the first through passenger train operated between Omaha and Portland.

The Oregon Short Line extended a number of branches in Idaho, completing the line to Hailey in 1883, to Ketchum in 1884, and to Boise in 1887. The terminal at Pocatello was a booming place and swarms of drifting "rails" hired out there long enough to make a stake. The accolade of a boomer rail was a service letter showing employment as Night Yardmaster at Pocatello, although it has been rumored that these service letters were dispensed on a cash basis by an unscrupulous Chief Clerk employed there.

The Oregon Railway & Navigation Company obtained the branch line built by the Northern Pacific into the Palouse in 1884. It had been built between Palouse Junction and Colfax in 1883. In 1885, the O.R.&N. extended it to Moscow, Idaho, and in 1886 built the Starbuck-Pomeroy line and the extension to Farmington. After Villard lost control of the road, the O.R.&N. opened the line to Spokane on October 7, 1889. They also built up the Snake River from Wallula to Grange City, Riparia, and Lewiston. The Heppner Branch was opened

November 26, 1888, with the last spike being driven by J. L. Morrow and Henry Heppner. Steel of the O.R.&N. also reached out from Tekoa to Harrison, Idaho, and on into the mining districts of Kellogg, Wardner, and Wallace.

The Oregon Railway & Navigation Company was leased to the Union Pacific in 1887, and was reorganized in 1896 as the Oregon Rail Road & Navigation Company. In 1910-11, another reorganization saw the road emerge as the Oregon-Washington Rail Road & Navigation Company, and today it operates under the shield emblem of the Union Pacific Railroad.

Under early Union Pacific control, efforts were made to extend the road from Portland to Puget Sound, through several subsidiary lines. These included the Portland, Seattle & Northern Railway and the Portland & Puget Sound Railroad, to be allied with the Great Northern. Some construction was actually done, but the project was halted in 1890. When the Northern Pacific and Great Northern united in 1905 to build the North Bank road, the Union Pacific jumped into the battle and renewed efforts for a Seattle line. This project culminated in a truce arranged in 1909 between the three roads, resulting in joint use by the Union Pacific and the Great Northern of the Northern Pacific tracks between Portland and Tacoma, beginning January 1, 1910.

The various lengths of trackage built by

Robert E. Strahorn's mysterious North Coast Railroad in eastern and central Washington during the early 1900's were gathered into the O-WR.R.&N. fold, revealing the true backers of the Strahorn projects.

The Union Pacific projected lines to Gray's Harbor in 1890 and again in 1905-09. When the truce was pledged with the N.P. and the G.N., the Union Pacific properties were granted use of the Milwaukee tracks into Aberdeen and Hoquiam.

The Arlington & Pacific Coast Railroad and the Columbia River & Central Oregon Railroad were both incorporated in 1903 to tap the rich Condon range lands. The O.R.&N. interceded and dirt was broken on September 13, 1904. Tracklaying began south of Arlington early in 1905, and the 44-mile Condon Branch was completed in May of that year.

The branch into the range lands of Harney County left the main stem at Ontario and reached Crane in July, 1916. This line was extended to Burns, where a pioneer mother, Mrs. Jennie Clemens, tapped home the last spike on August 16, 1924. A short branch left the Burns line at Vale to run up to Brogan. The story of the Shaniko trackage and the Deschutes Railway is told separately in this work.

Life was seldom dull along the original O.R.&N. line up the Columbia. Rocks rained down on trains passing the bluffs in the Gorge and sheep were a constant hazard in the sagelands east of The Dalles. The drifts of "blow sand" kept engineers alert and on the edge of their seat-boxes, for to hit these sand dunes was to invite derailment and disaster.

In 1891 a bad fire broke out in the business district of The Dalles and a wire was sent to Portland for help. A special train carried a fire engine on a mad dash up the Gorge, but arrived too late to be of much assistance. About 20 blocks of the city were completely wiped out. The engineer called to handle this fire special was "Blinky" Hoffman, one of the road's speed demons. With a clear track and orders to disregard the speed restrictions, Hoffman made a ballast-scorching run over the crooked track. Upon arrival at The Dalles, the entire crew was set up to a drink in the Umatilla House by Colonel McNeil, the Division Superintendent, whose private car had been coupled to the rear of the special.

Not long after the turn of the century, Fireman Art Sayre was down in the deck of a freight engine, bailing in the "black diamonds," as his train rambled east from Portland. He glanced up from his back-breaking task just in time to see his engineer dive out of the cab window on the right side, while the head "shack" left by the opposite opening. The puzzled fireman climbed to the engineer's seat and

BONNEVILLE DEPOT, complete with wooden station platform, is shown in this early view; men at right are handling prefabricated bridge timbers. Living quarters for station personnel occupied second story of station; one agent who resided here shortly after turn of century had three daughters who all worked regular shifts as telegraph operators, one of them later marrying a locomotive fireman on the road. (Courtesy of Union Pacific R.R.)

HANDWRITING ON THE WALL, the newly-laid tracks of the O.R.&N. were destined to send Columbia River steamboats to the bone-yard. Temporary construction spur runs down to boat landing in this scene in early 1880's; engine with "swallow-tail" tender is one of two O.R.&N. acquired from Pennsylvania Railroad. (Courtesy of Union Pacific R.R.)

PILLARS OF HERCULES, prominent Columbia River landmark, frames Engine No. 19 of the O.R.&N. Co. and a freight train. Photo clearly shows long pilot-bar coupler, used in the days of the treacherous old link and pin couplings.

looked ahead to discover the reason for the sudden flight of his crew. A glance showed a section of rail missing from the track and a section gang fleeing wildly from the gap. The engine hit the ties, tilted over, and slid down the bank, Fireman Sayre riding her to a stop and escaping uninjured. The section foreman had neglected to send out a flagman while his crew was removing a broken rail.

One of the serious accidents that occurred on the O.R.&N. was the collapse of the Eagle Creek bridge on February 2, 1890. The timber structure, weakened by flood waters, gave way when a locomotive and a caboose loaded with laborers was passing over it. The engine, with George Avery firing for Engr. Jack George, remained upright, but the tender and caboose dropped into the deep ravine. The death toll, as listed by the Portland "Oregonian," placed nine men killed and twenty-six injured. Among the dead were two O.R.&N. section foremen, Marithough and Casey. The crew had been bound from Cascade Locks to clear a big slide that was blocking the main line. A relief party was rushed down from The Dalles on one of the river steamboats belonging to the Company.

The "Navigation" part of the Oregon Railway & Navigation Co. was no idle phrase. The road operated a great many river boats, running on the lower, middle, and upper sections of the Columbia, as well as on the Willamette, Yamhill, and Snake rivers, and on Puget Sound. The railroaders on the line commonly referred to the River Division as "The Navy." The fleet of sternwheelers operated by the Oregon Steam

Navigation Co. had made the rail lines a reality, and, in return, the roaring wheels of the locomotives gradually forced the sloshing paddle-wheelers to the bone-yard.

Even as the steamers passed from the river, so did the memory of Henry Villard fade on the railroad he built. The old station of Villard, 7 miles east of Celilo, was renamed Grant's.

Grant's was a busy place for a time, as freight was ferried across the river to Columbus, Washington, but fire and floods ravaged the town and it wasted away to little more than a siding, today called simply "Grant" on the Union Pacific timetables.

Gone, also, are the old O.R.&N. veterans such as "Pa" Sherman, who started in the days of the original portage roads; Engineer George "Nig" Leech, who once rode his derailed engine to a watery halt in the swift current of the Columbia; Master Mechanic Dressel has long since departed from the smoky confines of the old Albina roundhouse, and the names of such runners as M. P. Wilkes, "Old Clinkerface," U. S. Hansen, "Stuttering" George Lang, Anson Curtis, and "Buck" Biblehausen no longer appear on the enginemen's register sheets.

Domed streamliners and Diesel freights speed

BRASS HATS AT HEPPNER. O.R.&N. officials line up for photographer in 1888. Engineer in gangway is John Patterson, who pulled first train over Heppner Branch. The big wind mill operated a pump to supply railroad's water tank. Crews to handle engines such as the 57 on official trips were usually hand-picked. (Photo from Ben Griffiths, courtesy of E. D. Culp)

FIRST TRANSCONTINENTAL TRAIN into Northwest on O.R.&N. tracks at The Dalles in 1883. Decorated locomotive, with stuffed cougar on pilot, stands in front of speaker's stand near New Columbia Hotel. Banner on stand reads "To The Atlantic," connection being made over newly-completed Northern Pacific R.R.; locomotive is O.R.&N.'s No. 46. (Courtesy of Union Pacific R.R.)

CABOOSE HOP. Engine 59 of the O.R.&N. displays the white flags indicating an extra train in this photo at Taylor, Ore., in 1908. Near Corbett, not far from here, "Old Bill" Miner robbed an O.R.&N. train in 1903 and eluded capture. A year later he robbed a Canadian Pacific train near Mission Junction, B.C., and in 1906 played a return engagement on the C.P.R., robbing the Transcontinental Express at Furrer, B.C. He was captured by the Northwest Mounted Police but escaped from the New Westminster penitentiary, was later captured in Georgia and died in prison there, after robbing a Southern Railway express train. (Courtesy of Fred W. Zirbel)

along the tracks where the fleet of little coal-burners rattled only a generation or two before. The little trains and the men who manned them have passed on, and even the memory of their trials and deeds is fading.

THE SNOW-BOUND EXPRESS

The month of December, 1884, saw raging storms sweeping the Northwest, blanketing much of the country with a mantle of snow. Early in the month, the Northern Pacific turned over the Pacific Express to the Oregon Railway & Navigation Co. at Wallula Junction. The Pacific Express was the plush overland limited of the day, and at this time consisted of seven cars, bearing about 150 passengers. Included in the consist of the Express was the St. Paul Pullman and another Pullman from the Dayton-Walla Walla Branch.

When the train arrived at The Dalles the storm conditions down in the Columbia Gorge were so bad that Supt. H. S. Rowe, head of the O.R.&N. at that point, caused the train to be held there for two days. On the morning of December 19th things had eased a bit and it was decided to try to run the west-bound Express on to the Portland terminal. The Express

was consolidated with another train that had arrived from Huntington, via Umatilla Junction, and went steaming away from The Dalles in charge of Conductor Edward Lyons. Two locomotives were used, one of them operated by the regular engineer of the Pacific Express, Charlie Evans.

All went well as the varnished cars clattered through Hood River, but about 2 miles west of Viento the engines slipped and bucked to a halt in the deepening drifts. The gale roaring up the Columbia buried the track behind the train, making it impossible to back the train up. The storm had knocked out all communication and it was some time before word of the stalled Express reached headquarters.

With the train locked securely in it's icy clutch, King Winter now unleashed a series of storms that froze the mighty Columbia River solid and spread drift upon drift deep in the Gorge. Aboard the stalled train, food supplies ran low and Big Ed Lyons struck out afoot toward Cascade Locks to obtain help for his marooned charges. He hired a number of fishermen to pack and sled food supplies to the hungry women and children, paying them $20 apiece for their services. On December 22nd

DELIVERY BY STEAMBOAT, this picture shows arrival of a small 2-4-0 type locomotive loaded on fore-deck of sternwheeler "HASSALO" at a landing on upper Columbia River. Wood scow, left foreground, hauled fuel from wooded areas and was sail-driven by strong winds.

he had sent off nearly all of the able-bodied male passengers, in an effort to conserve the rapidly dwindling food supply. These men walked down the Gorge in the teeth of the series of blizzards; some of them became so weak that they took refuge in farm houses along the way, and the remainder walked clear to Troutdale before meeting the relief train from Portland.

The Express was stalled under the high basalt bluffs that tower over the O.R.&N. tracks in this region, and the great gales of wind tore big limbs from the timber on the bluffs, pelting them down onto the helpless train. The crew chopped these limbs for fuel in an effort to heat the chilly cars.

The prospects for Christmas appeared grim for the 100-odd passengers on the marooned Express. Conductor Lyons led a human pack train up through the deep drifts from Cascade Locks, bearing additional food from the scanty supply on hand there. The menu for Christmas dinner consisted of bacon, beans, canned fruit, pickles, and coffee.

While the refugees huddled in their desolate coaches, the men of the Oregon Railway & Navigation Company were doing everything in their power to bring them relief. All of the available

labor in Portland was rushed to the western end of the Gorge and set to work digging at the frozen drifts. Even the city jail was emptied and the inmates sent up to aid in clearing the tracks.

A snow plow sent out from The Dalles was bucking the drifts toward Hood River when one of the locomotives overturned, and Engineer Hudson was killed in his crushed cab.

On December 30th, the big snow plow of the Northern Pacific arrived at The Dalles from Wallula in charge of J. M. Buckley, Western Superintendent of the Northern Pacific. This big plow reached Viento on the 31st of December and soon broke through to the rear of the

WASHOUT ON O.R.&N. dropped Engine 63 and caboose into ravine along Columbia River about 1890 with tragic results. Track walkers were used to patrol lines to prevent accidents such as this but were not always successful.

RAILROAD YARDS AT THE DALLES was scene of activity when this shot was taken, probably about 1890. Engines occupy 10-stall roundhouse at right, while a yard engine switches cars in foreground. Stock cars to handle sheep and cattle are being repaired on track to the right; large, white building beyond trestle in far left background is historic old 3-story Umatilla House, pioneer hotel whose fame was widespread. (Partridge photo, courtesy Union Pacific R.R.)

OLD STUB SWITCHES show in this view of Albina yard in early days. This type of switch moved ends of rail, which had to line up squarely with connecting rails, was in common use before invention of modern switch points. Dimly visible in the distance are the masts of sailing vessel at railroad dock. (Courtesy of Union Pacific R.R.)

ALBINA SHOPS were under construction when this photograph was taken in 1888. New roundhouse stands at right, behind water tank. The tall brick smokestack of powerhouse has long been a landmark in what is now Albina district of Portland. (Courtesy of Union Pacific R.R.)

RAILROAD CAR FERRY delivers a load of freight cars to switch engine at dock in Portland; first railroad bridge over Willamette River at Portland was not completed until June, 1888. Track at right was a 3-way stub type switch, shown here lined for cross-over. (Courtesy of Union Pacific R.R.)

. . . AND HIGH WATER. Flooding Columbia River sent drift swirling axle-deep around locomotives at The Dalles in 1894. Freight platform at left is stacked with bags of wool freighted in from distant sheep ranges for rail shipment. (Courtesy of Union Pacific R.R.)

WAITING FOR THE FLYER, station personnel lines platform at old depot at Umatilla. O.R.&N. lines branched here, one line going to junction with Northern Pacific at Wallula and south line to connection with Oregon Short Line at Huntington, via Pendleton. (Courtesy of Union Pacific R.R.)

JOHN DAY RIVER SPAN, this steel structure was completed about 1887, replacing original wooden bridge. River was named for John Day, a member of the Wilson P. Hunt party of Astor's fur company that came overland from the Missouri to Astoria in 1811-12; Day became separated from party in this desolate area, later made his way to Fort Astoria, lending his name to river and valley. (Courtesy of Union Pacific R.R.)

COLFAX INTERLUDE. Engine 62 of the O.R.&N. wisps steam from her cylinder relief valves as she idles before the Colfax, Washington, depot while passengers board her coaches. To right of engine can be seen the order board, arms of the semaphore-type signal indicate that telegraph operator has orders for the train. (Tecrasilk Photograph)

FIRST TRAIN INTO JOSEPH trails O.R.&N. Engine 113. Picturesque branch diverged from main line at La Grande, Oregon, and wound to Joseph in the beautiful Wallowa region via Elgin and Enterprise. (Courtesy of Union Pacific R.R.)

CLEANING UP after flood, about 1910, Oregon-Washington R.R. & Nav. Co. crew is shown at Colfax, Washington. Derailed cars behind pile of debris at right are property of the electrified Spokane & Inland Empire Railroad Company. Third and fourth from left are Fireman J. Hutchinson and Engineer Jack McCarthy. (Courtesy of J. E. Broyles)

BEARDED ENGINEER holds long oiler beside O.R. & N. Engine 46, a speedy 4-4-0 type, in this photo taken at The Dalles. Veteran runners Anson Curtiss, W. J. Sherman, Robert Hunter, Thos. Haslam, Don Dunlap, W. J. Graham, and others held the throttles of trim speedsters of this class of power. (Courtesy of H. H. Arey)

UNUSUAL VEHICLE at right is bicycle fitted with outrigger and flanged wheels, once used on O.R.&N. Contraptions were used for track patrol and were carried in baggage cars to enable a brakeman to pedal off for help in case train became disabled. (Courtesy of H. H. Arey)

CONNELL, WASHINGTON, was setting for this photo of O.R.&N.'s No. 113 taken about 1906. Engine was built by Manchester Loco. Works in 1883, had 55 inch drivers and was equally at home in freight or passenger service. (Courtesy of J. E. Broyles)

AT HOOPER JUNCTION, WASHINGTON, Engine 362 of the O-W R.R.&N. is being used in construction of the North Coast Railroad; the year, about 1912 or 1913. (Courtesy of J. E. Broyles)

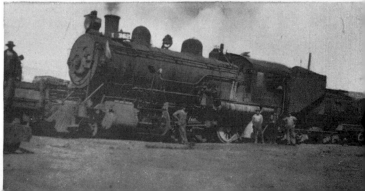

SMOKY SYMPHONY at LaGrande as bells toll and safety valves howl to the accompaniment of pulsating air pumps and roaring blowers. Diamond-stacked No. 761, at left, carries white flags to indicate she is running as an extra train, one without timetable schedule. Behind tank of Engine 383 can be seen incline tracks leading up to bunkers of coaling chutes. (Courtesy of H. H. Arey)

PLUME OF COAL smoke trails Ore. Ry. & Nav. Co.'s Eng. 84 as polished eight-wheeler streaks east from The Dalles about 1899. Passenger train is the Portland-Chicago Special, the forerunner of Union Pacific's "Portland Rose."

JETS OF STEAM FROM BLOWING WHISTLE hang suspended in air as the Portland-Chicago train wheels past mill of Bridal Veil Lumbering Company. The year is about 1907; engine is dashing ten-wheeler 134. (Courtesy of Union Pacific R.R.)

EAST OF LA GRANDE, a pair of coal burners send up a pillar of smoke and a shower of cinders as they shoulder into a stiff climb through sagebrush with early passenger train. (Courtesy of Union Pacific R.R.)

LENDING A HAND, the O.R.&N.'s No. 32 helps a cap-stacked eight-wheeler drag a string of passenger cars up the incline from the ferry slip at Portland; sternwheeler backing away from landing is the **"WILLAMETTE CHIEF."** (Courtesy of H. H. Arey)

POLISHED BOILER JACKET and straight-shot stack grace O.R.&N.'s No. 85, ready to leave Pendleton with a passenger train; hand-fired coal burner was a speedy eight-wheeler. (Oregon Collection, University of Oregon)

TOP END OF OLD "SHASTA LIMITED." Oregon-Washington R.R.&N. Co.'s Engine 201 carries indicators for Train No. 312. Southern Pacific operated the Shasta Limited as Train No. 12 from California to Portland, where it was turned over to O-W R.R.&N. to complete the trip north to Seattle. Big Pacific type helped maintain the fast schedule that made the "Shasta" a by-word for West Coast travel in its day. (Courtesy of H. H. Arey)

SHUNTING ENGINE of early days is typified by O.R.&N. No. 14, a saddle-tank 0-4-0. Short wheelbase allowed this engine to move dead locomotives around terminal shops and on turntables. Weight of water tank and entire engine on drivers gave added tractive effort. (Courtesy of H. H. Arey)

FANCY EIGHT-WHEELER No. 46 of the Oregon Railway & Navigation Co. stands on a trestle near Hood River in by-gone era. Pair of brooms fastened beneath headlight is believed to be a token indicating engine held record for fast running time over the road. (Courtesy of Union Pacific R.R.)

DEPOT AT MOSCOW (IDAHO, THAT IS!) marks end of Union Pacific branch that was operated as the Columbia & Palouse R.R. under proprietorship of Oregon Rail Road & Navigation Company. Men around Manchester-built No. 70 are, left to right, Engineer Fred Schnabel, Brakeman Jack McClain, and Fireman Glen Roberts. (Courtesy of J. E. Broyles)

AT WINONA, WASHINGTON, No. 72 couples onto a passenger train about 1910. Engineer is W. S. Walker; carman standing beneath gangway is L. D. Broyles. Carmen inspect running gear, air brakes, and other car appliances, are called "car-toads" or "car-tonks," also "car-knockers," "car-whackers," from act of tapping gear with hammers to locate defects. (Courtesy of J. E. Broyles)

IRON HORSE GETS A DRINK. Snappy No. 73 of the Oregon Railway & Navigation Co. was pulling passenger when this picture was taken at the Troutdale tank. (Photo from Ben Griffiths, courtesy of E. D. Culp)

NEW YORK LOCOMOTIVE WORKS, located in Rome, New York, built old No. 83 for the Oregon Railway & Navigation Company. The Rome works operated from about 1880 to 1895, turning out many fine engines such as this husky Consolidation-type freight handler.

ADMIRING LADIES gather with crew around old No. 9 of the O.R.&N. Engineers and conductors were glamorous figures in early days of railroading, rated at par with bankers and businessmen in social strata. The 9-Spot left the Baldwin factory numbered "3" but this road number had already been assigned to the former O.S.N. portage road engine, **"J. S. RUCKEL,"** so it was painted out upon arrival. Location of rear light atop cab proved unsatisfactory, was removed to rear of tender for improved visibility in backing up.

AN OUTLANDER, this lanky eight-wheeler bearing the Union Pacific legend on her cab is really No. 759 of the subsidiary Oregon Short Line. She was sent west to operate on the Pacific Division (O.R.&N.) lines from 1890 until 1893. (Courtesy of Union Pacific R.R.)

OREGON PORTAGE RAILWAY was built by the State of Oregon to assist steamboat operators to compete with railroad monopoly in Columbia Gorge. Road operated from 1891 until 1896; the 0-6-0 saddle-tanker shown here appears to bear the name **"ETTIE."** (Courtesy of the late R. V. Mills)

TOOLS OF THE TRADE. Posed alongside their O.R.&N. 10-wheeler, No. 130, the engineer holds a long oiler and the fireman leans on his hickory-handled scoop. Firing a coal-burner by hand was an art, and required skill as well as a strong back. Shovel was sometimes called a "banjo," perhaps because of the rhythmic scrape and clang as the fireboy bailed in the "black diamonds," playing a tune with his "arm-strong stoker."

A SEATTLE TRAIN, this is No. 361, hauled by a Pacific type locomotive, No. 205 of the Oregon-Washington Railroad & Navigation Co. Train is headed through a cross-over at a switch marking the start of double track. (Courtesy of H. H. Arey)

NEAT CONSOLIDATION TYPE, the 201 bears O.R.&N. initials on her cab panel, was used on the Snake River Valley Railroad, a 65 mile pike between Wallula and Grange City, Washington. Squared style firebox gave the boiler a distinctive appearance; type was called "Belpaire."

FINE EXAMPLE OF LONG-BARRELED TEN-WHEELER is this cap-stacked No. 75 of the O.R.&N., shown here on the turntable at The Dalles roundhouse. Firemen were responsible for keeping boiler jacket, domes, etc., cleaned and polished; wiper gangs in roundhouse cleaned running gear, rods, valve motion and tank.

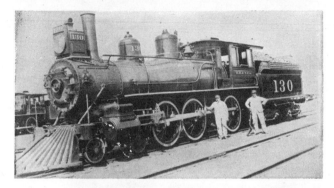

Iron Horses of the Dim and Smokey Past

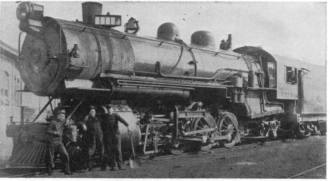

COLUMBIA GORGE PARADE. A photo story of the growth of motive power on the Oregon Railway & Navigation Company.

(No. 1) No. 20, an American Standard 4-4-0 at The Dalles, circa 1880.

(No. 2) No. 45, cap-stacked 4-6-0-, was built by Rome Locomotive Works in 1889.

(No. 3) No. 133, a Rome 4-6-0, after rebuilding by O.R.&N.

(No. 4) No. 209 was a 10-wheeler built by Brooks in 1908.

(No. 5) No. 215, slightly lighter than the 209, had larger drivers and higher boiler pressure, was built by Baldwin.

(No. 6) No. 194, big Pacific type, pulled passenger trains up the Gorge.

(No. 7) No. 440, a bulky 2-8-2 Mikado, handled freight drags east from Albina. Hand-fired, her tank held 20 tons of coal and she often used it all on the run up to The Dalles. (Photos 1 and 7, courtesy of H. H. Arey)

WEDGE-TYPE SNOWPLOW bolted on pilot of O.R.&N. Eng. 62 was used to clear tracks after blizzards. Four or five engines would be coupled on in rear and entire group roared into packed drifts with wide-open throttles. "Bucking" snow was dangerous as engines would telescope if derailed. Canvas atop tender protected coal supply from flying snow tossed by plow. Photo at The Dalles.

FAMILIAR SIGHT to Pacific Northwest railroaders in winter is ice-encrusted rotary snowplow. Locomotives pushed rotary along while steam from plow's own boiler furnished power to rotate blades and throw snow from tracks. This "spinning wheel" is halted in The Dalles, on the O.R.&N., about 1890 and is the prototype of snow-fighting equipment in use today.

DIGGING OUT DRIFTS on the Ore. Ry. & Nav. Co. line in the Columbia River Gorge during the snow blockade of 1884-85. Frozen snow defied efforts of primitive snow plows then in use and men were used to liberate the stranded Pacific Express.

stalled Express. The train was hauled back to Viento. The plow was run around it and proceeded to attack the blockade in the Gorge. On January 2nd, 1885, the Pacific Express rumbled into Bonneville on the heels of the plow, but the entire outfit was halted by a solid wall of snow and ice over the tracks between Oneonta and Multnomah Falls. The food supply at Bonneville was so scant that the Pacific Express was backed to Cascade Locks in order to obtain victuals for the weary passengers.

A crew of 1,000 men were busy hacking away with picks and shovels, but their progress was heart-breakingly slow. The big N.P. plow still battled the barricade, aiding the men in their efforts.

Then, as if no longer amused by tossing storm after storm upon the hapless rail line, Winter relaxed the icy clutch and sent a warming Chinook sweeping up the river. The ice thawed and the snow plows were enabled to buck the drifts aside. The relief trains from Portland broke through to a meeting with the Northern Pacific plow and the line was opened on January 7th.

In the black hours shortly after midnight, the Pacific Express reached Portland with it's

cargo of precious lives, saved by the courageous efforts of the valiant railroaders who had toiled to the point of complete exhaustion to liberate the train from the frozen trap. The grateful passengers were hurried off to their destinations and the railroaders went about their task of moving trains, unhonored and unsung . . . "all in a day's work."

THE SHANNON CONVENTION

One of the most unusual strikes in railroad history took place on the Oregon Railway & Navigation Company in the late 1880's and is embalmed in memory as the "Shannon Convention." The trouble all began when Supt. Cal W. Johnson departed for a vacation in California, leaving Mr. D. W. C. Perry in the post of Acting Superintendent. Perry set out to blaze a name for himself and the fire he kindled left a glow for many years. One of his first official acts was to attempt a wholesale rejuvenation of the O.R.&N. lines. He cut the wages of all operating train and engine crews 25%, eliminated about one-third of the operating personnel, and extended the length of the runs to be made by the road crews.

SNOW BLOCKADE RELIEF TRAIN on the Oregon Ry. & Nav. Co. during the terrible blizzards of 1884-85 posed long enough for photographer to expose his plate west of Hood River. (Courtesy of Union Pacific R.R.)

The O.R.&N. crews responded in a manner Perry never had expected. From the wilderness of the Blue Mountains, from the branch lines in Washington, from every place where the O.R.&N. turned a wheel, the crews deserted their jobs and began to converge on the terminal at Albina. Solid trains of cabooses rolled down the Columbia Gorge as the men headed for Portland to join in protest.

Headquarters for the strikers was set up in a hall over Jack Shannon's saloon in Albina and a locomotive engineer, Bob Hunter, was elected to head a committee representing the employees.

Jack Shannon was a former O.R.&N. conductor and his saloon was a favored spot with the "rails." To facilitate the speedy delivery of liquid refreshment to the thirsty members in the hall overhead a chute was rigged through the ceiling and a cow bell tied to a cord could be jangled to call for service. No violence marked the "strike" and for the only time in history practically all of the road's operating crews enjoyed a grand and glorious reunion.

Desperate over the turn of affairs, Acting Superintendent Perry sent a frantic telegram recalling Supt. Johnson, then sent a message from his Portland office to the strikers in Albina, across the Willamette River, requesting a meeting with the strike committee. That worthy body replied that, inasmuch as the fare on the Willamette ferry cost fifteen cents, it would be cheaper for Perry to come to them. Reluctantly, the Acting Super presented himself to the committee in session over Shannon's saloon and listened to the counter-proposal voiced by Engineer Bob Hunter.

The demands as set forth by the men were that the terminals of the freight runs remain at their former locations and that, instead of a 25% reduction in wages, the men be granted a 25% increase. Perry stalked huffily back to the ferry and the freight blockade continued to grow.

Meanwhile, a special on the Southern Pacific was blasting north over the Siskiyous, rushing Supt. Johnson back to Portland. When he arrived there he immediately granted the men's request and the satisfied "strikers" were dead-headed back to their far-flung terminals to resume their duties. History does not record the fate of the ambitious D. W. C. Perry, but the happy memories of the "Shannon Convention" never faded among the engineers, conductors, firemen, and brakemen who had gathered in Jack Shannon's saloon to defend their rights and partake of the cup that cheers.

BRANCH LINE FEEDERS
THE COLUMBIA SOUTHERN RAILWAY

DOWN THE GORGE, O.R.&N. Engine 80 wheels a passenger train. It was in such a locale as this that the Pacific Express was marooned during the great blizzard of 1884-85. (Courtesy of H. H. Arey)

This standard-gauge short line was built to serve the interior range lands of Sherman, Wasco, and Crook Counties of eastern Oregon. The Columbia Southern Ry. was incorporated by E. E. Lytle, J. M. Murchie, and D. C. O'Rielly on March 4, 1897, and proposed to build a railroad from Biggs to Prineville. The first survey was started on March 23, 1897, and actual construction began at Biggs, Oregon, on June 19th of that year. Biggs, or Biggs Junction, was a station on the O.R.&N. line about 20 miles east of The Dalles.

The road was completed into Wasco on October 6, 1897, and was well built, using 56 pound rails and good ballast. Depots and repair shops were also erected to serve the line, which was about 10 miles long.

On May 9, 1898, construction was started at Wasco on the southern extension, and at 5:30 P.M., December 14, 1898, the track gangs laid the rail up to the Moro depot, 26 miles south of Biggs, permitting Engine No. 1 to pull into town

ERUPTING A FOG OF COAL SMOKE, O.R.&N. 81 pulls away from the Hood River station, heading east. Building at left is depot of Mt. Hood Railroad. (Angelus Studio photo)

with a work train. Grading continued and the line reached south to Shaniko, the first construction train arriving there on May 13, 1900. Regular freight and passenger service between Biggs and Shaniko was inaugurated on May 15th.

The total length of the road was about 70 miles, including the short Hay Canon spur. It served the rich Wasco wheat region and the grazing ranges of Grass Valley and Shaniko.

The little road did a lively business, hauling supplies to the towns of Moro, Wasco, Grass Valley, and Shaniko; from the interior, loads of wheat, wool, cattle, and horses rumbled north to the O.R.&N. connection at Biggs.

The region served by the Columbia Southern was the locale for a lively range war that flared about the time the railroad was building. Cattle ranchers in the area resented the constant encroachment of sheep raisers on open range that the cattlemen claimed as their own. The cattlemen organized a secret group known as "The Crook County Sheep Shooters Associa-tion" and made a number of raids on sheep camps, frightening off the herders and killing large numbers of the "woolies." It was a number of years before these range wars were settled.

Shaniko, end of the Columbia Southern, was formerly called Cross Hollow. The name, Shaniko, is a corruption of the name of Mr. August Scherneckau, a pioneer settler on the site. The Columbia Southern erected their shops at Shaniko in 1902. The little road was later acquired by the Union Pacific interests and operated as the Shaniko Branch.

BRANCH LINE FEEDERS

In addition to the Columbia Southern Railway and the branch line to Heppner, a number of other branches and short lines connected with the Columbia River line of the Oregon Railway & Navigation Company.

The Dalles was selected as a terminus for a short line organized in 1898 by E. E. Lytle, D. C. O'Rielly, and W. H. Moore. These gentlemen

THREE GENERATIONS of Union Pacific power include little 1711, a ten-wheeler, Mikado type 2162, and big 2-8-8-0 type No. 3629, a heavy compound; coal chutes tower in background. (Angelus Studio photo)

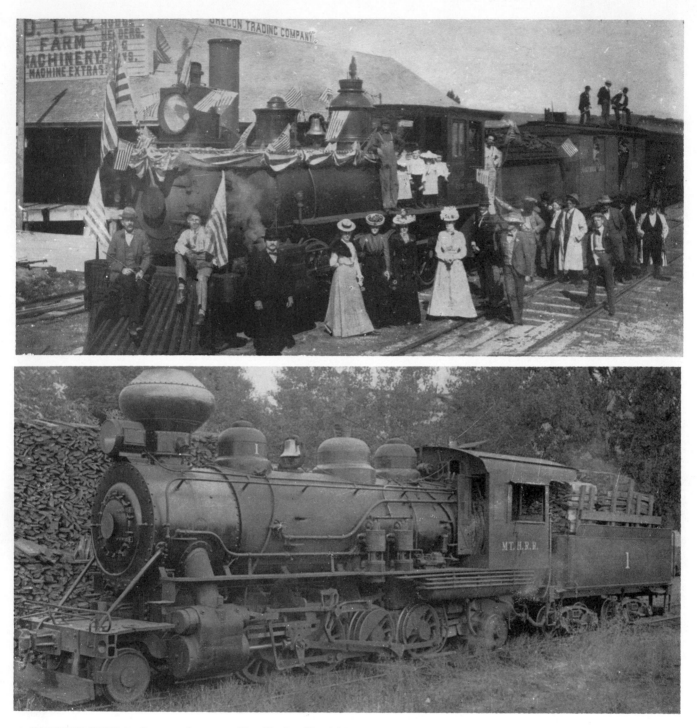

STETSON HATS in the crowd surrounding Engine No. 4 hint at the rangeland character of the region penetrated by the Columbia Southern Railway. Linen dusters on men at right protected the clothing of travelers, but mud and dust played hob with sweeping dresses of bonneted ladies.

SLABWOOD EATER was this bulky little Mikado type, the second No. 1 of the Mount Hood Railroad, shown here alongside the wood pile from which she was refueled. Rushton stack was especially designed for later woodburners, had a trap to catch and retain cinders. (Tecrasilk Photograph)

formed an incorporation known as The Dalles, Dufur & Des Chutes Railroad, to build south from The Dalles to Dufur and interior points. A survey for this road was completed in September, 1903, but nothing more was done. In 1904, the project was revived by the formation of a railroad named the Great Southern, and grading begun. The grading was completed between The Dalles and Dufur by April of 1905, and the final rails were spiked down into Dufur on September 18, 1905. The Great Southern served as a supply line to Jim Hill's forces dur-

SNAKE RIVER VALLEY RAILROAD'S 200 was a 2-8-0 built by Brooks. Note goat horns ornamenting headlight, and automatic coupler with slotted knuckle that could be used with link and pin equipment. Snake River Valley R.R. was a subsidiary of the Oregon Railway & Navigation Company. (Courtesy Oregon Collection, University of Oregon)

ing their drive up the Deschutes with the Oregon Trunk line a few years later. From Dufur, the Great Southern was extended about 11 miles south and west to Friend, in the timbered region between Tygh and Fifteenmile Creeks. In later years, this short line was abandoned.

Down the Columbia from The Dalles, another short line was extended into the Cascades from the town of Hood River. This line, the Mount Hood Railroad, was built in 1905 by the David C. Eccles interests in connection with his Oregon Lumber Company. The Mount Hood Railroad was built from a junction with the O.R.&N. at Hood River to Dee, Oregon, and later extended to Parkdale, a total distance of about 25 miles. The main source of traffic was

the big saw mill located at Dee; the first locomotive used on the road is reported to have been a second-hand Consolidation type obtained from the O.R.&N. This engine was a woodburner, as was later motive power on the road for many years.

In addition to the Mount Hood Railroad and the Sumpter Valley Railway, Eccles and associates built the Utah Pacific Railroad from Milford, Utah, to Uvada, on the Utah-Nevada state line. This 125-mile standard gauge road is now a part of the Los Angeles-Salt Lake line of the Union Pacific. In 1900, Eccles formed the Utah Construction Company, noted for railroad contracting throughout the west. In 1905 this company was given the contract to build the West-

OREGON & NORTHWESTERN RAILROAD is a short line with 51 miles of track, operating freight service only between Hines and Seneca, Oregon. The road connects with the Union Pacific at Burns, and its main traffic is timber products of Hines Lumber Co. O.&N.'s No. 5 is a slide valve Consolidation. (Chas. E. Kaine photo)

CAP-STACKED EIGHT-WHEELER is Central Railroad of Oregon No. 12. Engine was originally used on the Chicago & Alton Railroad. (Courtesy H. H. Arey)

COLUMBIA SOUTHERN RAILWAY No. 3 was a husky Consolidation type with powerful low drivers. Broom visible in front window of cab was wielded by fireman to clean cab floor and deck. (Courtesy of Union Pacific R.R.)

ON HEPPNER BRANCH, Fireman Arthur M. Sayre fills tank of No. 1725 at Ione in winter of 1915-16. Standing beside ten-wheeler are Brakeman "Chub" Davis and Engineer Jimmy Keane. (Courtesy of H. H. Arey)

UMATILLA CENTRAL RAILROAD, shownig Engr. "Dad" Moon at the throttle of first train into Pilot Rock, Oregon, Dec. 16, 1907. (Moorhouse photo, University of Oregon)

OREGON RY. & NAV. CO.'s 23 was a trim, three-domed American type coal burner. (Photo courtesy of Ben Griffiths)

ern Pacific Railroad trom Salt Lake City to Oroville, California. The job was to extend over 700 miles, and was the largest contract ever issued to a single company west of Chicago. Utah Construction Co. weathered the depression of 1907 and completed the Western Pacific in 1910. The continuous 1% grade for about 100 miles up Feather River Canyon is reputed the longest constant rail grade in existence.

Steel Trail West

MAIN STREET OF THE NORTHWEST

When the Overland route of the Union Pacific-Central Pacific lines was being projected to link the Atlantic with the Pacific, agitation was started for a similar rail line to link the Northwest with the Union. To carry out this venture the Northern Pacific Railroad received a charter signed by President Abraham Lincoln on July 2, 1864.

Financial problems and the Civil War delayed the work and the first earth was broken near Duluth on February 15, 1870. Indian troubles with the Sioux slowed construction and the road advanced slowly across the wind-swept Dakota plains.

There was a great deal of conflict in regard to the location of a terminus in the Pacific Northwest, with Seattle, Portland, Tacoma, and various other towns competing for the award. The Lake Superior & Puget Sound Company, representing Jay Cooke & Co., N.P. financial backers, selected a location on the Columbia River at Kalama, Washington, for the initial point of construction in the Northwest. The first ground was broken at Kalama in December, 1870, and the first spike driven there on May 15, 1871.

Contracts for construction north from Kalama were let to J. B. Montgomery and grading was carried on at various locations. Two locomotives were delivered to Kalama in October, 1871, and the work was accelerated. On September 7, 1872, the first train rumbled across the bridge over the Cowlitz River. By the time October spread it's haze through the timber, the rails had been laid into Tenino.

Tacoma was selected as the northern terminal in 1873 and the final spike was driven there on December 16th by M. M. McCarver.

Regular service began between Kalama and Tacoma on January 5, 1874, with steamboat and steamship connections at each end of the road. As traffic increased more locomotives were put on the line to aid the original motive power. The water supply of several of the original engines was so limited that it was found necessary to construct auxiliary water tanks on flat cars. These were coupled behind the engines by use of a pair of bent crowbars and they towered over the tiny locomotives.

The firm of Jay Cooke & Co. failed in the panic of 1873 and work on the Northern Pacific was at a standstill until 1875. The Northern Pacific Railroad was placed in receivership

HIGH CASCADES. A brace of early Northern Pacific engines, trailing a side-door caboose, shove a train of material into Stampede Pass tunnel during the construction of the N.P. line over the Cascades to Puget Sound. (Courtesy of Fred Jukes)

IN THE CLEAR. An early Northern Pacific 8-wheeler and a side-door caboose stand in a siding in the Cascade Mountains during construction of the road in the late 1880's. The funnel-stacked woodburner was a Baldwin product. (Courtesy of Fred Jukes)

SIDEWHEEL TRAIN FERRY, the "TACOMA" carried Northern Pacific trains across the Columbia River between Hunters Point (Goble), Oregon, and Kalama, Washington, before completion of the main line over the Cascade Mountains. (Courtesy of Northern Pacific)

RAILROAD RELIC. Northern Pacific's Engine 1, the **"MINNETONKA,"** was built by Smith & Porter in 1870. After service on eastern end of line, was shipped around Cape Horn and helped build western section. She was sold to Polson Logging Company, Hoquiam, Washington, in 1895, where this photo was taken. Discarded in 1928 and left to rust, she was purchased in 1932 by the Northern Pacific and restored. She starred in Chicago's "Century of Progress" and New York World's Fair, is now preserved by the N.P. in well-deserved retirement. (Courtesy of Northern Pacific Ry.)

PUGET SOUND TERMINUS of the Northern Pacific at Tacoma, Washington, in 1884. Sailing ships and sidewheel steamboat met trains at this wharf. Note N.P. box cars and stock pens on deck. (Courtesy Northern Pacific Ry.)

ON THE LAKE SHORE. Engine No. 2, the "D. H. GILMAN," served the Seattle, Lake Shore & Eastern Railway. Road was completed from Lake Washington to Sumas, on Canadian border, in 1891, later passed under control of Northern Pacific. (Courtesy of University of Washington)

MAIN STREET OF THE NORTHWEST, the Northern Pacific once owned a sizeable fleet of trim Standard, or American, type eight-wheelers such as old No. 280. Engines of this design were the speed queens of their day, but were replaced when they grew too light to handle the heavier cars that supplanted the old wooden coaches.

HENRY VILLARD, the shrewd old German who welded together a network of rails to form one of the great transportation lines in the Pacific Northwest. His famous "blind pool" is still a legend in financial circles, a coup that gave him control of the Northern Pacific. (Courtesy of Oregon Historical Society).

AMERICAN STANDARD. This 4-4-0 type, No. 13, was delivered to the Northern Pacific in 1871, and helped push back the frontier as the road stretched across the Dakotah hunting grounds, bound for the Pacific. (Courtesy of Northern Pacific Ry.)

45

STERNWHEELER "FREDERICK BILLINGS" carries Northern Pacific train across Snake River between Ainsworth and South Ainsworth, Wash. Ferry was in use from November, 1882, until Snake River bridge was opened on April 20, 1884. (Courtesy Northern Pacific Ry.)

when Jay Cooke & Co. became insolvent. Under Frederick Billings, the road was reorganized in 1875 but control was soon to pass into the hands of Henry Villard.

The Northern Pacific had resumed construction under the Billings regime, starting a line east from the mouth of the Snake River on October 2, 1879, and resuming work on the Missouri River end at the same time. By February of 1880 the road had 18 miles of track laid north of Ainsworth and the grade was completed into Spokane in September of that year.

Villard feared that the Northern Pacific would soon extend a connection along the Columbia River between Kalama and the Ainsworth section, competing with his Oregon Steam Navigation Company. To forestall such a move, he secretly set about gaining control of the N.P. lines. Early in 1881 he formed his famous "blind pool," asking friends to subscribe $8,000,000 for an unknown investment. He quietly bought up a controlling amount of Northern Pacific stock and, through his Oregon & Transcontinental Co., took over the Northern Pacific.

Work on the overland line was pressed, the

tracks from the east reaching Missoula in June of 1883. The western end had been completed to Clark's Fork on November 15, 1882, and Villard was rushing his new Oregon Railway & Navigation Co. road along the Columbia River. He also had organized the Astoria & Coast Railroad to build down the river from Portland to Goble, opposite the Kalama terminal.

The two ends of the overland tracks met on August 22, 1883. Villard planned a grand celebration to mark the completion of the Northern Pacific, so the last short gap of actual main line tracks had been left unfinished and trains routed around it by means of a "shoo-fly," or temporary by-pass.

The site of the ceremonies was to be at Gold Creek, Montana, some 58 miles west of Helena. A number of special trains were run from both east and west, bearing dignitaries and friends of Villard. Among the passengers on these specials were some of the nation's leading financial and transportation giants, including a number of European guests who crossed the Atlantic to attend the glorious moment.

Alas, for the best laid plans of mice and men! The grand celebration turned out to be a hilari-

PACIFIC GATEWAY, this is a scene on the Northern Pacific along the Clark's Fork River in western Montana in the 1880's. Old-fashioned hand pumper section car carries a crew of Chinese coolies, used in construction and maintenance. (Courtesy of Historical Society of Montana)

FAITHFUL OLD "NIG." This blaze-faced black horse was used to pull the 4-wheeled car that carried rail and ties from supply trains and dumps up to track-laying gangs of the Northern Pacific. "Old Nig" is reputed to have hauled these steel cars from Bismarck, North Dakota, to Gold Creek, Montana, where the crews from the east met those from the west. (Courtesy of Historical Society of Montana)

GOLD CREEK SPECIAL. One of the Northern Pacific engines that hauled the Villard special trains from St. Paul to the last spike ceremonies in Montana in 1883. The trim 8-wheeler has been polished and decorated with flags, bunting, and evergreens for the momentous occasion. (Haynes photo, courtesy Historical Society of Montana)

ous fiasco. The crowd that gathered at Gold Creek contained, in addition to the railroad construction crews, some 1,500 cowboys and miners, a band of Crow Indians, and the soldiers and military band from Fort Keogh, Montana. When Villard's influential guests began their flowery orations, the mob chafed and called loudly for General U. S. Grant, who was a guest but not listed for a speech.

So great was the clamor that Grant finally arose and made a five-minute response.

It had been arranged to have a track-laying race between the gangs from the east and west over the unfinished gap, the losers being required to stand the drinks to the winners. The gang from the west had the misfortune to derail a hand car used in moving rails and the crew from the east edged out Supt. John L. Hallett's crew by a slim margin of about 10 seconds.

Pandemonium reigned as the final rails clanged into place. The railroad gangs, numbering about 500 men, swarmed around the united ends of track, cheering, shouting, swearing, and draining bottle after bottle of "fire-water." Efforts to clear the mob away for the spike driving proved entirely futile and it was growing dark when H. C. Davis, a utility man from the North-

ern Pacific's Traffic Department, managed to pound home the final spike at 6:05 P.M. Not more than twenty of the guests of the road were able to penetrate the crowd to witness the act. It had been planned that Henry Villard would drive the spike but the unruly celebrants made it impossible. The spike driven at Gold Creek on September 8th, 1883, was a plain iron one and was the original first spike that had been used when the Northern Pacific was commenced near Carlton, Minnesota, in 1870.

Fifteen new locomotives were placed in service on the N.P.'s Northwest lines in 1883. Ten of these came overland and five were shipped out around Cape Horn. Haphazard operations often played havoc with motive power. Two locomotives had been seriously damaged in a head-on collision near Spokane early in 1882, an engineer and a fireman losing their lives.

To carry the Northern Pacific's trains across the Columbia, a sidewheel car ferry was built in New York, dismantled, and shipped to Portland on the "TILLIE E. STARBUCK." The 57,159 pieces were assembled at Portland in 1884 and the vessel was named the "KALAMA."

AS IT WASN'T! This painting depicts General U. S. Grant, with Henry Villard at his left, preparing to drive N.P.'s last spike in 1883. Orderly enactment of colorful ceremony was prevented by unruly mob of intoxicated spectators. (Courtesy of Northern Pacific Railway)

This ferry ran between Kalama, on the Washington side of the river, and Hunter's Point, on the Oregon shore. During floods, when part of the Astoria & Coast was under water, she brought trains from Kalama directly to the docks in Portland. In later years she was renamed "TACOMA."

The first refrigeration cars of the Northern Pacific arrived in Tacoma in October, 1883, loaded with 10 tons of live oysters shipped direct from Baltimore, Maryland. These succulent bivalves were packed in casks, each containing 45 gallons, and were kept alive by repeated drenchings with salt water. These cargoes came over the tracks of the N.P. to Wallula, thence over the affiliated line of the Oregon Railway & Navigation Co. to Portland. Freight destined for Puget Sound went on down-river to Kalama, then north to Tacoma.

To overcome this circuitous route, Villard projected the Cascade line of the Northern Pacific, to cross directly over the Cascade Mountains to Puget Sound. Tracklaying began at Ainsworth, Washington, on this extension in October, 1883, reached Prosser in November, 1884, and arrived in Yakima in December. The

rails entered Ellensburg on March 31, 1886, and were spiked down into Cle-Elum on December 3rd.

The rugged Cascade Range made such a barrier in the path of this extension that a temporary "switchback" was built to carry trains over Stampede Pass until a tunnel could be built.

The last spike on this new line was driven on June 1, 1887, and the first freight train left Tacoma for St. Paul the next day. The first train from the east arrived in Tacoma on June 7th. The Cascade tunnel was completed in 1888, as was the bridge over the Columbia at Kennewick.

The bridge across the Snake River on the old line between Spokane and Wallula was completed on April 20, 1884. Prior to this time, the N.P. trains had been ferried between Ainsworth and South Ainsworth by the sternwheel car ferry, "FREDERICK BILLINGS," commanded by Capt. William P. Gray. Later Capt. Gray had some major renovations made on the "FREDERICK BILLINGS" and used her ferrying cars for the N.P. between Pasco and Kennewick until 1888.

STEAM AND SAIL. Tall-stacked 8-wheeler No. 1 of the old Bellingham Bay & Eastern Railroad spots coal "jim-mies" for unloading at the bunkers on Bellingham Bay in 1892. At left can be seen empty "bunks" that have been unloaded at log dump, the logs floating in the boom in foreground. B.B.&E. hauled coal from Blue Canyon mine on Lake Whatcom, operating over part of the Fairhaven & New Whatcom street railway to reach this log dump and coal bunker. Road went into operation in 1892, extended to Wickersham in 1902, and was sold to the Northern Pacific in 1903. (Courtesy of Fred Jukes)

In addition to his job as captain of the ferry, William Gray ran a farm at Pasco and operated a boarding house where over 400 Northern Pacific employees were fed. When the N.P. graders attempted to build the Cascade line across Gray's farm without permission, the doughty swift-water skipper held them off with his loaded shotgun. The railroad officials were informed of the impasse and promptly telegraphed the $500 Gray demanded for the right of way.

Villard's Oregon & Transcontinental Co. had incurred too many financial obligations in construction of the Northern Pacific and other lines under it's control, and the empire fell apart. Villard resigned and the O.R.&N. slipped into the control of the Union Pacific. In 1887 Villard came back into the Northern Pacific's board of directors and was made chairman in 1889, holding this position until he retired in 1893.

During the late 1880's and through the 1890's, the N.P. extended it's system in Washington and Idaho by construction and acquisition of many miles of branch lines. The branch from Spokane to Palouse was in service on July 1, 1888. The Seattle & West Coast Railway was formed in 1887 and built about 14 miles of track from Woodinville to Snohomish before selling out to the Seattle, Lake Shore & Eastern Railway. This latter concern had been started by Seattle citizens in 1885. The Northern Pacific obtained control of the Seattle, Lake Shore & Eastern in 1890-91. Included in the Lake Shore properties were the Seattle-Snoqualmie branch, the Snohomish branch, the branch from Woodinville Jct. to Salal, and the 51-mile branch from Spokane to Davenport. This last branch was extended by the N.P. to Almira and Coulee City in 1890-93.

The Northern Pacific went into receivership in August, 1893, and was reorganized as the Northern Pacific Railway in 1896.

The Willapa Harbor branch was begun in 1890 as the Yakima & Pacific. The first train from Centralia reached Elma in January, 1891, and service was opened to Aberdeen in 1895. The line to Lewiston, Idaho, was built in 1898. Jointly with the Union Pacific, the N.P. formed the Clearwater region network which is presently operating as the Camas Prairie Railroad, serving Riparia, Lewiston, Orofino, Stites, Grangeville, Kamiah, Pierce, and Headquarters.

LONG BARRELED 349 was sturdy Northern Pacific ten-wheeler. (Courtesy of Fred Jukes)

NORTHERN PACIFIC'S 1149 was an American Standard formerly used on the Seattle, Lake Shore & Eastern Railway. The latter road acquired the Seattle & West Coast Railway in the late 1880's and both lines passed into control of the Northern Pacific in 1891. Note the headlight lens cover, hinged back against the side of the oil headlight housing. Engine was constructed by the Rhode Island Locomotive Works. (Courtesy of Fred Jukes)

FIASCO SITE. The pavilion erected at Gold Creek, Montana, for the last spike ceremonies. Note the crowd swarming over spot where rails met, and the photographers on the platform in left foreground. (Davidson photo, courtesy Historical Society of Montana)

The 5-mile long Craig Mountain Railway runs from the mill at Winchester to a connection with the Camas Prairie at Craig Junction, and nearby the little Nezperce Railroad leaves the Camas Prairie line at Craigmont for the 13.8 mile run to Nezperce.

Through the subsidiary Washington & Oregon Railway Co., the Northern Pacific built the line from Kalama to Vancouver in 1901.

The Washington Central Railroad, running 130 miles from Cheney to Adrian, was leased to the N.P. in 1898 for a period of 999 years.

The Oregon & Washington Territory Railroad, a system built by George W. Hunt in the eastern region of Oregon and Washington, fell into financial straits and was reorganized in 1892 as the Washington & Columbia River Railway. Control of this line, containing about 184 miles, passed to the Northern Pacific around 1898. It included the lines from Pendleton, Oregon, to Dayton, Washington, with branches to Pleasant View, Washington, and Athena, Oregon, and was known as the "Hunt Road."

In 1886, D. C. Corbin built a branch from Hauser Junction to Coeur d'Alene and a narrow-gauge line from the Old Mission to the near-by mines. Corbin sold his road to the Northern Pacific and the motive power from the narrow-gauge was shipped to Alaska during the 1898 gold rush.

The line from Tenino to Olympia was built under the charter of the Olympia & Chehalis Valley Railroad, a 15-mile long narrow-gauge that was converted to standard gauge in 1890.

The Northern Pacific continues to serve the region well, supporting it's slogan as "The Main Street of the Northwest."

The Experiences of an N.P. "Eagle-eye"

Engineer J. Harvey Reed was a pioneer locomotive runner when the Northern Pacific line was being pushed over the rough Cascade Mountains west of Ellensburg in the late 1880's. From the end of track at Easton, Washington, the rails climbed up the steep slopes by a series of switchbacks on a grade exceeding 3%. Two Decapod type (2-10-0 wheel arrangement) locomotives had been acquired by the N.P. to operate on this switchback and, at the time, they were reputed to be the heaviest locomotives in the world.

Engineer Reed was running a Baldwin ten-wheeler, No. 457, one snowy day in January and was called to take a car of heavy bridge timbers to Martin, at the foot of the switchback. The huge mountain engine was broken down when Reed arrived and Construction Superintendent Reardon urged him to take the car up with the little Baldwin. They began the ascent and negotiated the first "leg" of the switchback, but in backing up the second "leg" the sand pipes became plugged with snow. As the engine struggled up the next climb, her wheels began to spin and she slipped down, then began to run away back down the mountain. Unable to check

OLD SETTLERS, these Crow Indians gave a touch of color to the celebration marking completion of the Northern Pacific, invader of the hunting grounds of their tribe. Note the tomahawk held by the brave third from their right. Construction on the eastern end of the road was delayed by troubles with the Sioux, and a survey party up the Yellowstone in 1873 was guarded by 10 troops of the 7th Cavalry, led by General D. S. Stanley and Lt-Col. George A. Custer. (Courtesy Historical Society of Montana)

PLENTY OF OOMPAH! Henry Villard arranged for ample musical entertainment for his guests at Gold Creek. This plumed and nattily-uniformed military brass band made the Montana landscape resound with martial airs. (Haynes photo, courtesy of Historical Society of Montana)

her wild flight, Reed and his fireman jumped off into the drifts of snow lining the right-of-way. The engine and car hurtled down-grade like a rocket, careened out onto a high trestle, and plunged 75 feet into the gully below. A bridge man working on the trestle was killed and another escaped by a miracle, the engine tilting over his prostrate body in its wild fall.

Engine No. 457 was salvaged and put back in service and again Engr. Reed had a narrow brush with death in her steamy cab. About 4:00 A.M. on a March morning he was backing down the hill from Martin with the 457, without cars, and had an order to meet Eng. No. 222, Engineer Billy Atkinson, at Easton. Unknown to either of these men, the train dispatcher had issued them a "lap" order; Engr. Atkinson had orders to meet No. 457 at Martin. The two engines hit in the murky depths of Dingle's Tunnel at 4:48 A.M. Luckily, no one was injured, but the tender of the 457 was broken loose from the locomotive and the water all escaped. Reed had sufficient water in the boiler, so he and his fireman ran the 457 back up to Martin without any tender to report the accident. The sight of the "bob-tailed" engine, sans tender, caused quite

ENTRANCE TO STAMPEDE TUNNEL on Northern Pacific under construction in 1888; tunnel replaced old switchback over Cascades. Building in foreground housed power plant used in drilling long bore. (Courtesy of Northern Pacific Ry.)

FIVE LEVELS OF TRACK show in photo of Northern Pacific's "switchback" over Stampede Pass before completion of tunnel in 1888. (N.P. Ry.)

a stir among the railroad men who witnessed its arrival.

Reed ran the fast silk and tea trains on hot-shot express schedules between Pasco and Ellensburg, and later was given a passenger run between Ellensburg and Tacoma.

Death hovered over this brave "eagle-eye" on the night of Jan. 2, 1892, while descending the grade on the loops between Buckley and South Prairie. Running his passenger train at 40 miles per hour, he was horrified to see that a rail had been removed from the track ahead. He threw his train into emergency, then jerked the throttle wide open. This action caused the couplings to break and the locomotive, mail, express, baggage, and one unoccupied tourist car plunged over the embankment, while the rest of the train, including the occupied Pullman sleeping cars, slid to a safe halt. Reed was thrown out of his cab, but was not injured, nor were any other of the crew hurt seriously. The

wreckage burst into flames and by daybreak only a smouldering heap of ashes and twisted steel remained. The parties guilty of removing the rail were never apprehended.

Braking freight trains over the Stampede Pass in the early days was a hazardous job. The late Adelmer Price, of Seattle, was one of the N.P. freight brakemen who clubbed down handbrakes on this wicked mountain run shortly after the road was completed from Ellensburg to Tacoma. He related how the trainmen would go over their train before leaving Ellensburg in the winter. One brakeman would shovel the snow off the running-boards at each end of each car, while the others carried buckets of ashes and cinders to sprinkle on these bared places. When the train started down the steep mountain and the brakemen had to leap from car to car, applying and releasing brakes, these cindered areas gave them a fighting chance to land upright on the rocking, rolling cars.

All of this dangerous work at night was carried out under the feeble glow of the old oil hand lanterns, often undependable, while the winter winds whipped snow or freezing rain at the struggling trainmen. On their skill, and that of the engineer, hung the safety of the train as it plunged down the steep grades.

PASCO DAYS

Memories of early days around the Northern Pacific terminal at Pasco, Washington, remain fresh in the mind of Mr. Clement Wilkins, now living in Coeur d'Alene, Idaho.

"My family lived at Pasco in the early days. My father served for some time as watchman on the 'Frederick Billings' while the N.P. had her tied up at Pasco. The railroad was all there was there in those days. For two years I worked in the roundhouse during summer vacations. I got pretty handy at knocking down fires, hoeing ash pans, and filling boilers on those old-time four-driver locomotives, the old Portland type known as 'sage hens.' Later I quit the roundhouse and got a job as a station clerk, working at that for three years, then quit to go to school. Both of my younger brothers stayed with the railroad in train service . . . the older one, A. K. Wilkins, put in 51 years with the Northern Pacific. He died in the service and, at the time of his death, was the senior conductor on the Idaho Division of the N.P.; the younger one, M. P. Wilkins, quit the N.P. and boomed around for a while . . . 'Maggie,' as he was known, came over to the old Spokane & Inland Empire and was set up as a conductor when he was 21 years old. He quit there and was going to leave the railroad for good, but just could not get away from it. He finally settled down on the Union Pacific and put in some 35 years as conductor there. He died in uniform aboard a bus while on his way to the station to take out a passenger train. He was president of the Union Pacific

NORTH COAST LIMITED. Northern Pacific's ten-wheeler 300 drapes coal smoke over bracken fern near Goble, Oregon, shortly after fast flyer was first inaugurated in the 1890's. (Courtesy of Northern Pacific Ry.)

BIG TEN-WHEELER was Oregon & Washington Territory Ry. No. 9, the "Hunt Road." When rear side rods broke under wooden cab they frequently caused fatal injuries to enginemen on this type of power. (Ore. Collection, Univ. of Ore.)

'Old Timers Association' in Spokane at the time of his death.

"Three of my old Pasco schoolmates also became locomotive engineers."

The foregoing tells a story that was common in the early days of Northwest railroading. The railroad was a fascinating thing, what with it's noise, glamour, and speed. Schoolboys longed to grow up and run the shiny engines that hooted and chuffed through town, or they visioned themselves as daring freight "brakies," nonchalantly strolling over the rocking tops of the box cars. The passenger trainmen in their blue serge and brass buttons were the idols of some, while others pictured themselves at the throttle of the hotshots, cigar aglow and gauntleted hand resting carelessly on the cab armrest. The roads were expanding and the turnover in labor rapid; no wonder that many small town lads followed their boyhood heroes along the steel "Glory Trail."

EARLY NORTHERN PACIFIC. No. 684 a museum piece 8-wheeler handled Northern Pacific passenger trains years ago. (Photo, courtesy of Fred Jukes)

OILING AROUND. Engineer with long-spouted oil can performs time-honored task of anointing cross-head guides with "run-fast." (Photo by Henry D. Cole)

SNOWCLAD PEAKS and lofty Cascade Mountains tower over Northern Pacific's switch-back near Stampede Pass about 1888. Railroading over this steep grade was a man's job, especially in winter. (Courtesy Northern Pacific Ry.)

COEUR D'ALENE LINE. Northern Pacific's Engine 398 near Dorsey, Idaho. The wooden trestle is a rebuilding of an earlier one destroyed in a forest fire in 1895. Charred snags on hill are mute reminders of the devastating blazes that frequently swept through Northwest forests. (Courtesy of Northern Pacific Ry.)

Sage Brush and Rawhide

DOC BAKER'S PIKE

Probably no railroad in the entire Pacific Northwest will ever achieve the degree of immortality awarded the little Walla Walla & Columbia River Railroad that operated between Wallula and Walla Walla, Washington.

If other short lines merit the description of "two streaks of rust," this narrow-gauge pike could have been, and quite appropriately, referred to as "two streaks of splinters."

The road was the brain-child of a rather remarkable pioneer, Dr. Dorsey Syng Baker. Reared in Mt. Carmel, Illinois, Dorsey Baker was a graduate of Jefferson Medical College in Philadelphia. He made his way west to the vast Oregon Country in 1848, opened a store and doctor's office in Portland, and made a jaunt down to California. Shortly after his return to Portland, he married Caroline Tibbetts,

daughter of pioneer Gideon Tibbetts.

Baker freighted merchandise to the Yreka mines with ox teams and established a flouring mill in southern Oregon.

In 1858, he moved his family to the little settlement of Walla Walla, Washington Territory.

Although partially handicapped by a stroke while on a stage coach, returning from one of his trips back east, Dorsey Baker was soon a leading figure in the Inland Empire.

He opened a store in Walla Walla and gathered a sizeable herd of beef cattle to range over the bunch grass knolls. The miners of the region brought so much gold dust to Baker's store for safe-keeping that Baker and his brother-in-law, John Boyer, sold the store and opened Washington's first bank.

This bank was later managed by one of the doctor's sons, Will Baker. At birth this son

HISTORIC WASHINGTON LOCOMOTIVE is this little 0-4-0 tank engine built by Porter, Bell & Co. in 1872 for the narrow-gauge Walla Walla & Columbia River Railroad, where she bore the name **"WALLULA,"** the second piece of motive power on Dr. Baker's pioneer line. She was sold to the Columbia & Puget Sound Railroad in the 1880's and worked around the Seattle yard until 1897. In 1905 she was again sold, this time to a logging railroad. Photo shows her when she was in service on the Columbia & Puget Sound as their No. 7. Her twin sister, W.W.& C.R. No. 1, the **"WALLA WALLA,"** was sold to J. W. Sprague in 1881 and used in constructing the Northern Pacific Railroad.

ONCE COMMON SIGHT on the railroads of the Northwest, the old covered wooden bridges are now nearly extinct. They protected bridge timbers but were susceptible to fires set by engine sparks.

The directors decided upon a slim-gauge line to hold down construction costs, and President Baker had another ace up his sleeve. Having seen the portage lines at the Cascades in operation, he planned to use wooden rails to conserve the road's cash. Baker made a trip to the Atlantic Coast, and stopped in Pittsburgh to order two locomotives for his 3-foot gauge road. These little monsters were both 0-4-0 types, weighing about 7½ tons each. They burned wood and carried their water supply in a tank atop the boiler. The order for these two engines was placed with the firm of Porter, Bell & Company. Engine No. 1 was named the "WALLA WALLA" and No. 2 became the "WALLULA."

Actual work on the line was started at Wallula and a gang of men were employed on the upper Yakima River, cutting logs to be driven down to the saw mill at the Wallula landing. This mill was in charge of Dr. Baker's son, Frank, and turned out the ties and wooden rails for the initial track.

Doc Baker had the reputation of being a "driver," and the construction crews complained about their working conditions and the food supplied in their mess. A strike was organized, and Baker discharged the ringleaders, but did hire a new set of kitchen personnel and the food improved.

The wooden rails were faced with strap iron by the crews under Truax, and the road crept steadily eastward; soon the two locomotives arrived and began to draw work trains out to the end of track. Soon after the arrival of the engines, Baker received a shipment of conventional rails manufactured in Wales, and these were used to replace the strap-ironed wooden

was christened Walla Walla Willie Baker, but in later years he adopted the more dignified name of W. William Baker.

The town of Walla Walla was growing rapidly, but was handicapped by the lack of speedy transportation. The nearest shipping point was Wallula, about 30 miles distant.

Dr. Baker set out to remedy this bottleneck, and in December, 1868, a charter was issued to the Walla Walla & Columbia River Railroad. An attempt to get Walla Walla County to back the bond issue was defeated by a narrow margin, so Baker and his associates set out to build the road with what cash they had on hand. The survey for the line between Walla Walla and Wallula was made by Major Sewall Truax, and the route was a feasible one, with easy grades and light excavation work.

NEW LUXURY FOR PASSENGERS was this coach built by Billmeyer & Small at York, Pennsylvania, for the Walla Walla & Columbia River Railroad. It replaced the box cars fitted with wooden seats formerly used, and was named "BAKER" in honor of Dr. Dorsey Baker, president of the slim-gauge Washington pike. Car was constructed about 1876.

stringers on the curves and on the steeper grades, where wear was the heaviest.

The panic of 1873 slowed construction, but by the end of 1874, the tracks had been laid to Whitman Station, only 10 miles short of the Walla Walla goal. The many economies practiced on the struggling pike gave rise to some of the tallest tales ever to emerge from the Northwest. Some of these were printed in book form, and a number have actually become widely accepted as the unvarished truth. The tale was spread that the wooden stringers were surfaced and bound in place with that ever-present frontier commodity, raw-hide.

Local wags spread the yarn that the hungry coyotes gnawed the rawhide in the winter months, causing the track to disintegrate; these, and other outright fabrications still enjoy some circulation.

In the strap iron days, the train speeds were slow and frequently the trains were delayed by "snake-heads" caused by the straps breaking under the weight of the engine or cars, then curling up to pierce the car floors. To economize, the road built no water tanks for some time, and the crews "jerked" water from the trackside streams with buckets to replenish the supply. Great herds of cattle ranged the bunch grass hills and often strayed onto the unfenced right of ways. To help keep them run off the tracks, Frank Baker trained a sheep dog that rode on the train and dashed ahead to send trespassing cows flying away with indignant bellows.

At first, no passenger cars were provided and travellers rode on top of the sacks of grain loaded on flat cars.

The road did have a passenger car in operation not long after the regular service started. This first car was nothing more than a box car with wooden benches built along each wall. The early cars were built at Wallula from local lum-

OLD SETTLER IN WASHINGTON TERRITORY was this tiny teakettle built by Porter, Bell & Co. in 1876 as the **"COLUMBIA"** for old Dr. Baker's Walla Walla & Columbia River narrow-gauge line. Engineer is busy screwing down rod cups to lubricate bearings in this photo taken at Walla Walla about 1903 when engine belonged to O.R.& N.; note the old style "hay burner" oil lanterns held by three trainmen. (Courtesy J. E. Broyles)

UP-GRADE THROUGH THE PINES, No.'s 7 and 8 of the Sumpter Valley Ry. boost a log train and trail a passenger coach. Note link and pin coupler on leading flat car. (Courtesy Oregon Historical Society)

ber, using trucks and fittings shipped out from the East.

The home-made coach was locally called the "Hearse."

The main traffic over the Walla Walla & Columbia River line was wheat, ton upon ton of it, and the road piled up an enviable record of earnings, but incurred the hostility of the ranchers by charging high freight rates. Old Doc Baker, shrewd in all business deals, sold six-sevenths of the capital stock in the road to the Oregon Steam Navigation Co. in 1878. A year later, he sold the remaining interest to Henry Villard, who changed the road to standard gauge in later years. A short narrow-gauge connection was built from Walla Walla to Dixie and operated as the Mill Creek Flume & Manufacturing Co., later becoming the Mill Creek Railroad. Two of the Baker road engines were used on the Mill Creek Railroad.

In addition to the original "WALLA WALLA" and "WALLULA" the road acquired four more Porter locomotives. These were named the "COLUMBIA," "BLUE MOUNTAIN," "MOUNTAIN QUEEN," and "J. W. LADD."

Old Doc Baker, appearing as fierce as a Biblical prophet with a snowy beard that nearly reached his belt, pocketed a tidy sum estimated at over one million dollars from his sale of the Walla Walla & Columbia River Railroad. The subsequent owners, the Oregon Ry. & Nav. Company, disposed of the power when the road was widened to standard gauge. Engines 1 and 2 had been sold previously, the first to a contractor building the Northern Pacific in 1881 and the second to the Columbia & Puget Sound. The other engines were sold, one going to the Cascades Railroad and later to the Ilwaco Ry. & Nav. Company.

No record remains of the disposal of No. 6, the "J. W. LADD." Old settlers around Wallula have a hazy recollection that one of the Baker road engines, sold to a logging road in Oregon or Washington, jumped the tracks at the terminal while being shipped, and fell into the river. She was reportedly left there, slowly becoming buried in sand. If this story is true, perhaps this was old No. 6, now sleeping out Eternity beneath the backwaters of the McNary Dam. Born out of demand for faster connections with the steamboats of the Columbia, it is fitting that her final resting place is beneath the deep waters of the River of the West.

POLYGAMY CENTRAL

One of Oregon's most picturesque short-line railroads has become only a memory, with the passing in recent years of the Sumpter Valley Railway. The 3-foot gauge line was organized in 1890 to build west from Baker into the ma-

jestic Blue Mountains, it's primary purpose being to tap the rich stands of pine timber and the mines of the region.

Guiding light of the Sumpter Valley was David C. Eccles, a Scot born in Paisley, Renfrewshire, in 1849. His family joined a group of Latter Day Saints and migrated to Salt Lake City in 1863. Young Eccles was soon started in the lumber business, and it was the lure of the great virgin stands of pine that led to his Oregon venture.

In addition to the slim-gauge railroad, the Eccles interests formed the Oregon Lumber Company to handle the timber. Since Eccles and most of his associates from Utah were members of the Church of Jesus Christ of Latter Day Saints, or Mormons, it was only natural that the local wags should dub the railroad the "Polygamy Central." As this proved rather offensive to those of more delicate sensibilities, the road

WOOD SMOKE IN THE PINES. A passenger train on the Sumpter Valley Railway poses on the trestle near Alder Springs, with pine timber forming a park-like backdrop.

soon was nicknamed "The Stump Dodger," an appropriate sobriquet for the winding length of narrow-gauge trackage.

Construction started at South Baker in 1890 and the road obtained a second-hand locomotive from the Utah Northern to handle the work train. This engine was a Grant 8-wheeler and bore the road number 285, a number that the Sumpter Valley never bothered to change. The new grade reached out from Baker to Salisbury, where it turned up the canyon of the Powder River. The track was laid into McEwan in 1892 and soon trains of logs were rumbling down to the Oregon Lumber Company mill at Baker.

In 1895 an extension was started that reached Sumpter in late 1897, following the original survey made by Joseph A. West. The Oregon Lumber Company erected a sawmill at Sumpter, and fragrant loads of fresh-cut pine lumber trailed the diamond-stacked wood-burners down to Baker.

In addition, the Sumpter Valley carried an increasing load of passengers and general freight. Gold mines pocked the mountains and a smelter flourished in Sumpter to reduce the precious ore into bars of bullion.

In 1901, the Sumpter Valley again thrust a steel artery toward the sunset, building an extension slightly over 14 miles long to the new terminal of Whitney. The new track climbed steep grades and wound around sharp curves to Larch, then dropped down to the North Fork of the Burnt River.

A later extension in 1904 saw the steel climb the grade to Tipton and down the steep slopes to Austin and nearby Bates, where the Oregon Lumber Company established another sawmill.

Terminal facilities for the railroad were erected at Austin, including a four-stall enginehouse.

The final westward push of the Sumpter Valley was begun in 1909 and the extension completed in 1910, carrying the rails over the hump at Dixie and down to Prairie City. Dixie station was located at the highest elevation on the entire line, being 5,238 feet above sea level.

Although the timber thinned out west of Dixie, there was a concealed purpose in Eccles' extension into Prairie City. It is known that Eccles hoped to build a connection to the narrow-gauge Nevada-California-Oregon Railroad, then in operation between Reno and the end of track, which finally terminated at Lakeview, Oregon.

While David Eccles traced his projected routes over maps of Oregon's great cattle ranges, his slim-gauge engines continued to boost tonnage over the humps between Prairie City and Baker. Slab wood from the mills was customarily used in the fireboxes of the locomotives, and firemen such as Melvin G. Hutchins, a long-time veteran on the road, tossed literally mountains of it into the flaming maws of the iron colts.

The earlier rails were light and soon became badly worn, and derailments were frequent. One freight pile-up near Whitney overturned a string of stock cars, allowing many of the cattle to escape. When the Prohibition Age smote the land, the Sumpter Valley unwittingly aided a moonshiner who shipped his "white mule" over the road in regular 10-gallon milk cans.

The Sumpter Valley had a great variety of motive power in operation on its 80-mile main stem. Early records on the road's locomotives were destroyed, but the roster once included 4-4-0's, 2-6-0's, and a couple of 2-8-0's. Starting in 1915, the road acquired a 10-wheeler and five 2-8-2 Mikado types, built by Baldwin Loco. Works and the American Loco. Company. These engines were equipped with the Rushton style, or "cabbage-head" smoke stacks.

An odd addition to the roster was a geared Shay acquired in 1897.

Most of the earlier engines were purchased second-hand, coming from such roads as the Utah Northern, Chateaugay Railroad, Tonopah Railroad, and the Eureka & Palisade.

In 1940, the Sumpter Valley disposed of wood and began to use oil for fuel. This was largely brought about by the acquisition of two big articulated engines purchased from the defunct Uintah Railway, formerly serving the gilsonite mines out of Mack, Colorado. These engines were side-tankers, with a 2-6-6-2 wheel arrangement and were real power plants. The Sumpter Valley removed the side tanks and placed tenders behind the new giants.

These big freight haulers displaced the smaller "Mikes" on the run between Baker and Bates, the 20 miles of track from Bates to Prairie City having been abandoned in 1933. Passenger service over the remaining line was discontinued in 1937. The end of the "Polygamy Central" came about in 1947, when all service was ended and the company began to dispose of its rolling stock.

Engines 19 and 20 had been sold to the White Pass Route in 1941.

Engines 16, 17, 18, and 50 were sold to the Peruvian Government in South America.

The two articulated engines, No.'s 250 and 251, were dismantled in 1947, shipped to Portland, and loaded aboard the S.S. "COASTAL ADVENTURER." They were taken south for their new owners, the International Railways of Central America, and are reported in operation out of Guatemala City.

Today, the mule deer browse under the pines, undisturbed by the thunder of Sumpter Valley locomotives, and the clear atmosphere of the Blue Mountains is no longer perfumed by the tantalizing aroma of pungent wood smoke and exhaust steam.

PITCH SMOKE CURLS UPWARD from the diamond stack of No. 17, a Mikado type built by Baldwin in 1915 for the 3-foot gauge Sumpter Valley Railway. Her tender piled high with pine slabs, she is ready to buck the steep grades of the Blue Mountains west of Baker, Oregon. Engine was later sold to the Peruvian Government.

Canadian Corridor

UP THE FRASER
(Canadian Pacific Railway)

Surveys for the Pacific Coast end of the Canadian Pacific were begun in 1871 and extended through historic, rugged regions. Civil engineers sighted their instruments on landmarks that had witnessed the passage of the noted explorer, David Thompson, in 1807. The roaring mountain streams that boiled white in the many canyons had echoed the chants of the voyageurs of the old Hudson's Bay Company as the fur brigades had passed through the country.

The colorful Sandford Fleming was Engineer-in-chief of the C.P.R. at this time and he wisely selected Walter Moberly to locate a route east from Burrard Inlet, not far from present-day Vancouver, B.C.

The extremely rugged terrain in northern British Columbia, coupled with the rigors of the climate and the hostile attitude of the native Indians, was responsible for the final selection of the Burrard Inlet route.

Contracts for 127 miles of railroad were then let to a brilliant young American engineer, Andrew Onderdonk. Backing Onderdonk's venture on the C.P.R. construction was a syndicate formed by D. Ogden Mills, Simeon G. Reed, W. B. Laidlaw, and L. P. Morton.

From Port Moody, on Burrard Inlet, to Emory's Bar the work was under the supervision of Canadian Government Engineer Marcus Smith; another Government Engineer, Henry J. Cambie, supervised the rugged Fraser Canyon section from Emory's Bar to Boston Bar.

Onderdonk established his headquarters at Yale, B.C., and his wife presided there as a perfect hostess, entertaining the dignitaries and engineers who were interested in the road.

The difficult construction tasks and the acute supply problem were not the only diversions that occupied Onderdonk's mind. Labor

CANADIAN PACIFIC trestle at Eight Mile Creek was a timber structure 67 feet high. The side cut beyond was 160 feet deep, passing under rocky spire. Supply road bridge can be seen through timber at far left in this photo made during construction in early '80's. (Courtesy of Canadian Pacific Ry.)

CANADIAN PACIFIC STEEL creeps eastward through Lower Fraser Valley in 1881. Funnel-stacked locomotive in rear pushes cars of material to laborers who carry ties and rail ahead to form track. Terrain became rugged when line reached Fraser River Canyon and a large number of Chinese were imported to labor on construction. (British Columbia Provincial Archives)

was not plentiful in that remote region and the first crews of graders were composed largely of ill-fitted miners that had failed in the rush to the Fraser mines. This segment of humanity contained a great deal of riff-raff and some criminal element, all eager to put in their time for the going wage of $2.00 per day and up. Most of this undesirable element drifted on after acquiring a stake, and Onderdonk imported large numbers of Chinese to labor on the grades.

While Onderdonk was blasting a path up the Fraser, work was being pushed on the eastern portions of the C.P.R. under other difficulties. A bridge of extra-length ties laid across the ice on the Red River allowed the C.P.R. locomotive "John G. Haggart" to steam into Winnipeg, much to the delight of 6,000 spectators.

Major A. B. Rogers, a New Englander, was engaged about this time to locate a pass through the jumbled Selkirks, and a more colorful character would be difficult to find. Rogers was a short, snappy little man with Dundreary whiskers and a masterful command of profanity, the latter to such an extent that he was nicknamed "The Bishop." Dressed in overalls and armed with a plug of his favorite "chawin' terbaccy" and a sea-biscuit for inner nourishment, he set out from Kamloops with a compass and an aneroid, accompanied by Indian guides and after a couple of attempts he discovered the pass that still bears his name.

While Major Rogers was probing the desolate Selkirk Range Andrew Onderdonk's army hacked their way up the Fraser. About 7,000 men signed his pay roll and toiled along the line. In the 60-odd mile section between Yale and Lytton they bored 15 tunnels, one of them 1,600 feet long. So rugged was the nature of the canyon that men were lowered by ropes

A JOB WELL DONE. Donald A. Smith (Lord Strathcona) drives home the last spike of the Canadian Pacific Railway at Craigellachie, B.C., on Nov. 7, 1885. Gent in top hat with square-cut white beard is Sandford Fleming, civil engineer. Site is in Eagle Pass, discovered by Walter Moberly. He followed an eagle's flight through the gorge between Shuswap and Hunter ranges to locate route for the C.P.R. main line. (Courtesy of Canadian Pacific Ry.)

OCEAN TO OCEAN, proclaims the banner on the side of Canadian Pacific's No. 374. The occasion is the arrival of the first train to enter Vancouver, B.C., in 1887, when an extension of the C.P.R. created a new terminal, replacing old Port Moody. Engine's headlight bears a portrait of Britain's Queen Victoria. (Courtesy British Columbia Provincial Archives)

to drill holes for blasting in the sheer rock walls. All supplies had to be packed in on horses and mules, creating such a problem that a plant was set up between Emory and Yale to manufacture dynamite on the spot. Onderdonk determined to build a steamboat to run up through the Grand Canyon of the Fraser to operate on the navigable waters above.

The craft was constructed by a master shipwright, William Dalton, and was named the "Skuzzy." She was a sternwheeler 120 feet long, with a 20-compartment, watertight hull. In addition to her powerful engines that cranked her paddles, she had a steam winch or capstan placed on her bows, driven by two engines, to enable her to "line over" the rapids. Onderdonk secured the services of Captains S. R. and David Smith, notable white-water pilots from the Columbia River in Oregon. Capt. S. R. Smith, with Engr. J. W. Burse and a crew of 17 men, successfully hauled the "Skuzzy" through Black Canyon and Hell Gate, arriving in a battered

but serviceable condition at Boston Bar. The trip had taken two weeks and the hardest battle with the roaring currents of the Fraser had

"SKUZZY," sturdy sternwheeler, battles the rock-studded torrents of the Fraser River. Steamer was built for Andrew Onderdonk to haul supplies used by his crews engaged in constructing western end of Canadian Pacific. (Courtesy British Columbia Provincial Archives)

TWO QUEENS MEET. Canadian Pacific's Engine 363 brings a passenger train along the landing of the sternwheeler, NAKUSP, on the upper Columbia River. (Courtesy of British Columbia Provincial Archives)

FROZEN COLUMBIA RIVER at Robson, British Columbia, presents frigid appearance in this 1899 picture; sternwheeler in background moves a locomotive, aboard a barge, downstream from Lower Arrow Lake. The little **"ILLICILLEWAET"** in the fore breaks ice away from rail ferry slip. Tracks on opposite shore lead away toward Okanagan Lake and the Kettle Valley region; Great Northern's branch from Spokane to Republic, Washington, connects with C.P.R. west of here at Grand Forks, B.C. (Courtesy of British Columbia Provincial Archives)

CLATTERING AROUND SWEEPING CURVE, a three-car passenger train trails steam in chilly atmosphere as it hurries to meet the old sternwheeler **"SLOCAN"** at Rosebery, British Columbia, on Slocan Lake. Barge at ferry slip is loaded with freight cars being transferred by tug. Passenger train from Nakusp unloaded travelers here for steamboat ride to Slocan City, where connecting train picked them up for trip into Nelson, B.C. (Courtesy British Columbia Provincial Archives)

CANADIAN PACIFIC LOCAL pulls away from sternwheeler **"NELSON"** at a landing on Kootenay Lake. C.P.R. steamboats made connections with company's trains at three points on the lake, Lardeau, Kaslo, and Procter. (Courtesy of British Columbia Provincial Archives)

ARRIVAL OF FIRST SCHEDULED TRAIN of the Canadian Pacific Ry. at Port Moody, B.C., July 4th, 1886. This original terminus was located at east end of Burrard Inlet, on a wharf 1,370 feet long. Terminal was removed to deeper water at Vancouver in 1887. (Courtesy of Canadian Pacific Ry.)

occurred at China Riffle; here, in addition to the powerful thrust of her big sternwheel, the steam winch, and a crew of 15 men at a capstan, it was necessary to enlist 150 Chinamen tugging on a third hawser to line up over the rapids.

While the grade crawled east up the Fraser, the line from the east was steadily coming west. The treacherous muskeg bogs on the eastern end swallowed up rails and ties, and in one bad spot three locomotives sank out of sight forever. Construction in the eastern approach through

BLACK CANYON OF THE THOMPSON RIVER, with a C.P.R. construction train. Between Port Moody and Savona's Ferry, 10,600,000 cubic yards of rock and earth were removed by pick, shovel, powder, and nitroglycerine to prepare the roadbed. Work was performed by Andrew Onderdonk's crews. (Courtesy Canadian Pacific Ry.)

the mountains was managed by a Cromarty Scot, James Ross. By the end of 1883 the railroad was at Laggan, on the summit of Kicking Horse Pass. The camp there was called Holt City, after Herbert S. (later Sir Herbert) Holt, a young Irishman employed by Ross as Chief Engineer. The men employed by Holt were mostly Finns and Scandinavians, the Finns usually proving to be the best hard-rock men. Drilling was done during the open season of the year, while the winter months were spent in cutting timber for ties and bridges.

A tense moment befell Holt in his quarters near Beavermouth. The C.P.R. was often in perilous financial straits, and at the time of the Beavermouth incident the wages due the crews were 13 months overdue. The crews struck and started to raid Holt's camp but that worthy faced them down, backing his stand with a Winchester rifle.

To help maintain order in the rough construction towns along the line, the Government stationed Mounted Police at various points. Close supervision was kept over the gamblers and saloon keepers who flocked after the labor gangs, eager to prey on the hard-working construction "stiffs."

MAGNIFICENT TIMBER TRESTLE supports a passenger train of the C.P.R. on the scenic Kettle Valley Railway in the southern part of British Columbia. (Courtesy of Canadian Pacific Ry.)

ON THE "BIG HILL," Canadian Pacific's No. 315 poses with officials and two business cars in 1890. Upper track at left is a safety switch spur, used to halt runaway trains by heading them up a steep incline if crews lost control when descending mountain. This old line between Hector and Field, B.C., was partly replaced by the famous Spiral tunnels and an easier grade. (Courtesy of Canadian Pacific Ry.)

Major Rogers was fond of the bottled variety of nourishment and believed that plenty of bacon and beans, served three times a day, was ample for his staff. The crews under James Ross varied their diet with beef from the herds of Pat Burns, Canadian cattle baron, and Rogers' men often found an excuse to visit the Ross forces around meal time.

The Onderdonk forces completed the line from Port Moody east to Savona's Ferry in July of 1885; the extension from Savona's Ferry to Eagle Pass was finished in September. The railhead from the east crept over Rogers Pass and the two ends of track met at Eagle Pass. The last spike ceremonies were extremely sim-

FIELD INTERLUDE. Rangy Mogul No. 73 of the Canadian Pacific and her crew pose for the camera at Field, B.C., foot of the famous Field Hill. In the late 1880's, her engineer was very fond of her and Fireman Arthur Randall called her the "Pride of the Valley." The Brotherhood of Locomotive Firemen formed Gold Range Lodge, No. 341, on this part of the C.P.R. and held regular meetings at Kamloops. (Courtesy of Fred Jukes)

ple. The event took place without fanfare at Craigellachie on November 7, 1885. Donald A. Smith, guiding light in the C.P.R. venture, drove the final spike, a plain iron one of the type used in the construction. His first blow bent the spike, and Roadmaster Brothers replaced it with another; this one Smith carefully tapped into place, with Major Rogers "sniping" the tie in position. The first spike, which had been bent, was tossed aside and was pocketed by Sir William C. Van Horne's secretary, Arthur Piers.

Called on for a speech, Van Horne replied, "All I can say is that the work has been well done in every way." The conductor then called "All aboard for the Pacific!" and the first transcontinental train in Canada rumbled west toward Port Moody.

Aboard the private car, Smith told young Piers to hand over the symbolic spike, saying he wished to use it for souvenirs. He had it split into bands and mounted with diamonds as presents for ladies connected with the party.

Missing at the last spike driving was Herbert Holt; he was busy with the task of repairing track in the notorious "Gumbo Cut" west of Revelstoke. His crew managed to stabilize this sink hole enough to permit the special train's passage, but the schedule was so arranged that the dignitaries passed over it at night in order to conceal it from their sight.

In 1887 the C.P.R. was extended from Port Moody for an additional 13 miles into Vancouver, B.C., the first transcontinental passenger train arriving at the foot of Granville Street on May 23rd.

Completion of the Canadian Pacific's main line to the eastern provinces was merely the initial thread in its network of rail lines in British Columbia.

One pioneer railroad on Vancouver Island was the Esquimalt & Nanaimo Railway, which was chartered in September, 1883. This standard-gauge line extended north along the eastern side of Vancouver Island, the 78 miles from Victoria to Wellington being opened in September, 1886. The control of the Esquimalt & Nanaimo Railway was acquired by the Canadian Pacific and the road leased to the C.P.R. but operated under its own name.

Under Canadian Pacific control, the road was expanded with a westward branch to Lake Cowichan and another westward branch, located further north on the island, that carried the trains into Port Alberni; from the Port Alberni branch a spur runs north to Great Central.

North from Wellington, the road built up past Union Bay to the end of track at Courtenay. The Esquimalt & Nanaimo played a vital role in the development of Vancouver Island.

LADNER CREEK BRIDGE, on the Canadian Pacific's Coquihalla line in southern British Columbia. Deep gorges and sheer bluffs created a big task for the railroaders who built this tough mountain division. (Courtesy of Canadian Pacific Ry.)

MISSION JUNCTION MEET. A pair of Canadian Pacific 10-wheelers were caught by Photographer Fred Jukes at this British Columbia junction point in 1902. Engine 441, at left, is pulling the Vancouver-Seattle passenger; locomotive at right is a sister engine, No. 442. (Courtesy of Fred Jukes)

ESQUIMALT & NANAIMO'S ENGINE 1, shown here at Shawnigan Lake on Vancouver Island. Deer horns decorate her big oil headlight. (Courtesy of Ernie Plant Collection)

BALDWIN TEN-WHEELER was the second locomotive on the Esquimalt & Nanaimo to bear the number 1. Flanged cap on "straight-shot" stack was ornamental. (Courtesy of E. White collection)

ISLAND EXCURSION. Decorated Engine No. 5 of the Esquimalt & Nanaimo Railway is coupled to a load of happy excursionists. Shown in the photo are baggage-combination car No. 3 and coaches 7 and 8. (Courtesy of Ernie Plant collection)

STURDY ISLANDER. Engine 10 of the Esquimalt & Nanaimo handled trains over the rugged Malahat Mountain grade. The little road is a subsidiary of the Canadian Pacific and operates on Vancouver Island, British Columbia. (Courtesy of Ernie Plant collection)

THE INVADERS

For many years after the completion of the Canadian Pacific Railway envious eyes had been cast on the great undeveloped potential of northern British Columbia and the lucrative traffic carried by Canada's first transcontinental. A number of schemes were planned to push competing railways into the vast domain, but it was not until after the turn of the century that any actual work began.

The Grand Trunk Pacific Railway Company was chartered on October 24, 1903, for the purpose of constructing a transcontinental rail line across Canada, the Western Division to extend from Winnipeg to some point on the Pacific Ocean. The road had the backing of the Dominion Government, and the first sod was turned in Manitoba Province in 1906.

Survey parties for the Grand Trunk Pacific swarmed through the rugged region watered by the upper Fraser, running through the historic Hudson's Bay post of Fort George. In 1908, when the surveys were taking form, three Grand Trunk Pacific officials toured the proposed route from Edmonton to Prince Rupert. These gentlemen were B. B. Kelliher, the chief engineer, Bob Lett, colonization agent, and C. C. Vanarsdol, chief engineer for the western district from Edmonton to Prince Rupert. Vanarsdol is credited with being the man who actually located the route of the road through the mountain region.

The road pushed slowly west from Edmonton, and reached Mile 53, near Tete Jaune Cache, late in 1912. A severe setback had occurred in April, 1912, when Grand Trunk Pacific's President Charles M. Hays went down with

FROM SOUTH OF THE BORDER came this early Consolidation type, built by Baldwin in 1884 for the Canadian Pacific. No. 313 was used on Field Hill and Kicking Horse Pass, in the Canadian Rockies. (Courtesy of Canadian Pacific Ry.)

CANADIAN RELIC. No. 374 hauled the first Canadian Pacific train into Vancouver, B.C., in 1887. Built in C.P.R. shops at Montreal in 1884, she was restored and recently presented to the City of Vancouver. (Courtesy of Canadian Pacific Ry.)

CANADIAN PACIFIC RAILWAY built this Consolidation type, No. 401, in 1886 under the direction of Chief Mechanical Engineer F. R. F. Brown. She was the first 2-8-0 type built by the C.P.R. shops and is shown here at Nelson, B.C., in 1902. Engine was scrapped in 1922. (Courtesy of Fred Jukes)

VANCOUVER TERMINAL was the setting for this shot of Canadian Pacific's No. 442, a trim ten-wheeler, in 1902. Company-built in 1889, she had an all-metal cab with countersunk rivets, resulting in a smooth exterior finish. (Courtesy of Fred Jukes)

CANADIAN PACIFIC'S No. 668, shown here at Vancouver, B.C., was a company-built 10-wheeler and sported the Pittsburgh system of two-cylinder compound steam distribution (Courtesy of Fred Jukes)

the ill-fated liner, "TITANIC." His vacancy was filled by Edson J. Chamberlin.

From Tete Jaune Cache, fleets of scows were soon booming down the turbulent upper reaches of the Fraser, loaded with supplies for the railroad contracting firm of Foley, Welch & Stewart. A supply depot for these supplies was established at Prince George, just above the mouth of the Nechako River.

The tracks of the Grand Trunk Pacific marched steadily toward the western ocean, passing under the shadow of Mt. Robson near the Tete Jaune, or Yellowhead, pass. This peak, highest in the Canadian Rockies, had an elevation of 12,972 feet.

On January 27, 1914, the track-laying machine "PIONEER" crossed the Fraser River on a temporary piling trestle to bring the steel into Prince George. A celebration was held, complete with speeches and band music, while the mercury hovered at 8 degrees below zero.

Construction from the western end of the Grand Trunk Pacific had also been under way, with the steel leaving the salt water at Chatham Sound and following up the north bank of the Skeena River through Terrace and Hazelton. The two ends of track met, the final spike was driven, and the first through passenger train rolled into the Pacific terminus of Prince Rupert B.C., on April 9th, 1914.

Due to heavy construction costs and losses incurred during the first World War, the Grand Trunk Pacific was taken over by the Canadian Government in 1920 and is operated today as a part of the Canadian National Railways.

Although there was scarcely enough business to support one road, competition was not long in coming. The Canadian Northern Railway was formed in July, 1899, by the combina-

GRAND TRUNK PACIFIC steel creeps west in 1908, as track layer strings ties and rails ahead of construction train. Broad plains are eastern approach to the torturous mountain terrain that lay ahead. (Courtesy of Canadian National Rys.)

ELEVATING GRADER, drawn by teams at right, loads earth into dump wagon as construction crew makes a cut on the Grand Truck Pacific's main line. Picture was taken in September, 1906, when this equipment was stylish for railway building. (Courtesy of Canadian National Rys.)

FRAME SHACKS AND TENTS housed construction gangs of Canadian Northern at Chu Chua, B.C., near Kamloops, when rails were being pushed west to Vancouver. (Courtesy of Canadian National Rys.)

BUNDLED AND BEARDED, this hardy gang of surveyors run their lines through the snow while doing location work for rail lines in British Columbia that became a part of the Canadian National Rys. system. (Courtesy Canadian National Rys.)

BOUND FOR PRINCE RUPERT, this is Engine 112 of the Grand Trunk Pacific hauling one of the first trains over the road through the desolate north country. (Courtesy of Canadian National Rys.)

PRINCE RUPERT LINE pioneer, this tiny locomotive was used in construction of the Grand Trunk Pacific's steel highway to the western ocean. (Courtesy of Canadian national Rys.)

tion of a few short lines in the northern district of the Prairie Provinces. Expanding, the Canadian Northern was in operation from Winnipeg to Edmonton by 1908, and soon the steel was reaching west.

For miles the Canadian Northern followed the Grand Trunk Pacific so closely that the crews blew cinders into each others' eyes. However, after crossing Yellowhead Pass, the Canadian Northern swung away to the southwest and dropped down to Kamloops, then followed the Canadian Pacific down the swift waters of the Fraser to Vancouver.

The Canadian Northern was completed by 1915, but was soon in financial difficulties. It was taken over by the Canadian Government in 1917, but operated under it's own name until 1919, when it became a part of the Canadian National Railways. The line of Canadian Northern is operated today as the Kamloops Division of the Canadian National system, while the former rival road in British Columbia, the old Grand Trunk Pacific, is the Canadian National's Smithers Division.

The line from Yellowhead Pass to Prince Rupert played a vital role during the last war. The operating officials had ample reason to be grateful to Charles Hays and his engineer, C. C. Vanarsdol. Hays insisted on a first-class railroad, built properly from the start, and Vanarsdol's surveys gave Hays the easy grades he demanded.

At some date in the future the line may prove a vital link in the much-discussed railroad to the interior of Alaska.

LONELY OUTPOST
(Pacific Great Eastern)

Deep into the vast northern wilderness of British Columbia a steel trail wends its torturous way along narrow mountain shelves and across yawning chasms. For over forty years this lonely mountain pike was known as the road "that began nowhere and ran to no place," but recently all that has been changed.

Advertised as the "Railroad with a Personality," the Pacific Great Eastern Railway was incorporated under a British Columbia charter on February 27, 1912. The original object of the road was to provide a link from Vancouver, B.C., north and east to Prince George on the new Grand Trunk Pacific. Much of the cash for the road came from the Great Eastern Railway in England, from which the Pacific Great Eastern derived its name.

One of the first steps in construction was the purchasing of the Howe Sound & Northern Railway, a 10-mile pike running north out of Squamish, in 1912. Work was also started on a line from North Vancouver and the grading crews were at work on the east end of the acquired Squamish line, headed for Prince George. By 1914 the line from North Vancouver had reached Dundarave in West Vancouver, but the outbreak of the World War brought work to a halt on this section.

The road languished until 1918, when the British Columbia Government acquired the capital stock and poured new life into the P.G.E. The rugged section from Squamish to Quesnel was opened for traffic in 1921. This 347-mile segment of track was isolated from physical connection with any other railroad. Freight and passengers arrived at the Squamish docks by barge and steamer to commence the journey inland. Traffic was light and in 1929 the North Shore branch out of North Vancouver was discontinued; the main stem from Squamish to Quesnel continued to run trains over the rough track, connecting with the company's barge line and steamers of the Union Steamship Co. at Squamish.

The scenic grandeur along the P.G.E. attracted considerable tourist traffic and the P.G.E. obligingly sawed the top off a passenger car to provide an open-air, sightseeing observation coach. Travel over the road was accomplished in a leisurely manner reminiscent of by-gone days. The steam locomotives screeched around the sharp curves under the skilled hands of such colorful engineers as Charlie Midnight, slowing to permit passengers to view the moose and other wild animals that frequented the right-of-way.

The twin ribbons of steel provided the great

TRACK-LAYING MACHINE at work on Pacific Great Eastern Railway near Alexandria, B.C. Ties from cars behind locomotive and rails from cars ahead of it are moved forward by conveyors. Men in foreground are placing ties while group in front of machine are placing and spiking down rails. Locale is not far from Quesnel, end of P.G.E. line for a number of years. (Courtesy of British Columbia Provincial Archives)

FIRST TRANSCONTINENTAL of the Canadian Northern pauses on the drawbridge at Kamloops, B.C., on its way west to Vancouver. (Courtesy of Canadian National Rys.)

interior with a link with the outside world, but the supporters and personnel of the P.G.E. never ceased dreaming of a real connection with other rail lines. The dream began to materialize when World War II boomed the business of the region. Work was started in 1949 on an 80-mile extension from Quesnel, which the road had hopefully dubbed a "temporary terminus" for nearly 30 years. This extension connected with the Canadian National at Prince George in 1953 and, at long last, the P.G.E. had a steel tie with the outside world.

More recently, the extension from Squamish south to North Vancouver has been pushed to completion and work is under way on a new extension from Prince George to Fort St. John.

All this new construction brought back fond memories to C. R. "Charlie" Crysdale, a veteran civil engineer who helped build the original Squamish-Quesnel section of the Pacific Great

Eastern. Chief Engineer for the P.G.E. during the 1912 construction was Pat Callahan, an ex-Canadian Pacific employee, and during the peak of construction over 4,000 men were at work along the line. Many of these were Montenegrans, refugees from the troubled Balkans, while the balance were mainly Swedes and Italians.

In an interview published by the Vancouver Herald in their "P.G.E. Development Issue" of August 25, 1956, Charlie Crysdale states:

"I surveyed from boats on the water, from trees, hanging from ropes, (and) on small rock ledges. Damn near killed myself several times" but allowed he had "more fun out of that cockeyed enterprise than in anything else I've done." When the extension was planned from Quesnel to Prince George, Crysdale and a crew set out to locate a feasible route; in his crew were some of the top engineers in Canada. However, Crysdale states that it was an alcoholic Alberta trap-

VICTORIA & SIDNEY RY. was opened between these cities on Vancouver Island in 1895. Photo shows Engine No. 3 of this short line. (Courtesy of E. White collection)

82

CANADIAN PIONEER. Engine No. 1 of the Howe Sound & Northern was a British product originally used on Vancouver Island. The Howe Sound & Northern was the fore-runner of the Pacific Great Eastern. (Courtesy of Ernie Plant collection)

GLORY IN THE MUD. One of the last spikes of the Grand Trunk Pacific is driven home at Mile Post 1372.7 on April 7th, 1914, while crowd of construction men happily watch the simple ceremonies. (Courtesy of Canadian National Rys.)

per and mink rancher, W. O. Greening, who located the best pass. "This man was a genius," says Crysdale, "I've never seen anyone who had the native gift for finding routes as much as he did. Off with another trapper he went, and in a few weeks he came back with the answer." The route, over the Cottonwood River, still stands and Greening now has a station on the Pacific Great Eastern named in his honor.

Steeped in the lore of the Cariboo, climbing through magnificent scenery, the Pacific Great Eastern is now busy helping to carve out a new Northwest Empire, and is no longer the lonely little pike in the wilderness.

OREGON CENTRAL LOCOMOTIVE on bridge over Clackamas River near Oregon City. Destruction of this bridge by flood nearly cost loss of land grants when road was racing to complete first 25 miles of track to comply with land grant terms. (Courtesy of Southern Pacific)

East Side, West Side

TWO OREGON CENTRALS
(O&C-SP)

In this day of regimentation and endless controls the situation that existed in Oregon in the 1860's would not be tolerated, but in those turbulent, lusty days anything could happen. Oregon was developing, and her growing pains were aggravated by the lack of transportation. The ocean voyage to California was hazardous, and the jolting stage coaches took six days to make the run from Portland to Sacramento.

Men of vision dreamed of an iron highway to the south, and several railroad projects were afoot. Promoter Joseph Gaston put a survey party in the field, led by A. C. Barry and George Belden, to locate a route from Jacksonville to the Columbia River. While the surveyors plodded along with rod, chain, and transit, political pressure was brought to bear on Congress, resulting in an act that provided for a land grant. Under the terms of this act of 1866, twenty alternate sections of land per mile were to be given to the railroad company that was granted the franchise. The joker in the deal was that the state legislature was to designate the company to receive the grant and the franchise.

Gaston and a group of Oregon citizens formed the Oregon Central Railroad Company and the state legislature passed an act designating the Oregon Central as the recipient of the franchise to construct a railroad from Portland to the California state line and to receive the vast land grant.

This plum was too juicy to escape notice and in a short time a rival faction, headed by a promoter named S. G. Elliott, formed the Oregon

SLOW BUT SURE, Chinese with pick and shovel load one-horse dump carts while hacking out Ore. & Cal. R.R. grade in 1872. Local newspapers, referring to white labor bosses, remarked that they were "herding Chinamen." (Courtesy of Southern Pacific)

GAUDY FLYER. Cars of this Ore. & Cal. passenger train were painted canary yellow. The place is the bluff above the Willamette River near New Era, the year, 1870. Man standing by stump in foreground is H. Thielsen, Chief Engineer, who located many miles of early Northwest rail lines. (Courtesy of Southern Pacific)

HISTORIC MOMENT. The first spike of the East Side Company's Oregon Central Railroad is pounded home in East Portland on October 28, 1869. (Courtesy Oregon Historical Society)

BRIDGE GANG AND PILE DRIVER stand on temporary span over Cow Creek during relocation of Ore. & Cal. R.R. tracks destroyed by "Big Slide" of 1890. (Courtesy of Southern Pacific)

THIS, TOO, WAS A PART OF RAILROADING. Teamster prepares to leave a warehouse with wagon-load of supplies for construction crews when Oregon & California Railroad was building extension from Roseburg to Ashland, 1881 to 1884. Man with thumbs in vest is Peter B. Whitney, Commissary Supt.; three Chinese in group are interpreters and labor bosses for large numbers of Chinese employed on road. Railroad furnished large amounts of rice, a staple in their diet. (Courtesy of Mrs. Don Whitney)

BIG SLIDE OF 1890 WROUGHT HAVOC on O.&C. main line in Cow Creek Canyon. Main body of slide was about 150 ft. deep, over 1,000 ft. long, covered an estimated 40 acres. Crew here works on relocated line; original track is buried on opposite side of creek. New track cut through part of slide, had 2 new tunnels, and was about 4 miles in length. (Courtesy of Southern Pacific)

Central Railroad Company of Salem, thus putting two Oregon Centrals in the field.

The original company favored a route down the west side of the Willamette River, while the Salem outfit planned an east side line. The West Side road broke the first ground at Portland on April 14th, 1864 and on the 16th of the same month the East Siders turned their first sod on Gideon Tibbetts' farm in East Portland. After a great deal of legal hocus-pocus, and very little progress, construction work was suffering when Ben Holladay, the western transportation magnate, secured an interest in the East Side road.

Ben Holladay was no waster of time, and soon had forced Elliott out of the organization. Holladay's cash backing and high-pressure operations were put to work and soon the state legislature revoked its grant to the West Siders and handed it over to the Oregon Central of Salem.

A provision of the grant called for 25 miles of track to be completed by January 1st, 1870 and work was rushed on the grade south from East Portland.

A second-hand locomotive was shipped out from the Michigan Central Railroad and arrived in Portland aboard the bark, "WEBFOOT," in November of 1869. After nearly being lost in the river during unloading, the Hinkley wood-burner was christened "J. B. STEPHENS" and soon was shoving work trains to the end of track. Gangs of Chinese laborers were busy with shovels and wheelbarrows, while crews of axemen cleared a path through the dense timber.

Ships delivered cargoes of rail and machinery and a saw mill was built to supply timbers for bridges. It appeared that the first 25 miles would be completed in time to meet the deadline, but in November a sudden freshet washed away the Clackamas River bridge. Holladay purchased a primitive locomotive from the Cascades portage road and hurried it by steamer to continue grading beyond the gap while crews hastily rebuilt the demolished bridge. The span was replaced and the first train chugged across on Christmas Day, 1869. A special conveyed the commission appointed to examine the track over the completed section and it was accepted. The rough spots in the hastily-laid line were smoothed out by heavy applications of Holladay's stock of champagne.

With the land grant safely locked in his safe, Holladay pushed construction and reorganized the road into the Oregon & California Railroad.

Grading gangs, consisting largely of Chinese laborers, were strung out at various locations, and the trains were soon running to Salem, then Albany, and on to Eugene.

Holladay obtained control of the West Side Oregon Central and extended it up the west side of the Willamette; trains reached Cornelius in 1871 and the line was extended to St. Joseph, on the Yamhill River, in 1872.

In order to clinch his monopoly in western Oregon, the bearded old "King of Hurry" organized the Willamette Transportation Co. in 1871 and operated nine steamboats on the Willamette and Yamhill rivers.

One of Holladay's first acts had been to discharge the chief engineer employed by S. G. Elliott. This man, T. R. Brooks, was reportedly addicted to the over-consumption of alcohol, and he was replaced by John Flint Kidder, later to achieve fame as the president of California's Nevada County Narrow Gauge Railroad.

New locomotives began to arrive, including the "OREGON," "PORTLAND," "CLACKA-MAS," "SALEM," and "ALBANY", for the east side main line. Over on the west side, Engineer W. W. Scott was handling the latch and Johnson bar on the "JOHN H. COUCH," an ex-Pennsylvania Railroad locomotive; she was soon joined by a second locomotive named the "DALLAS."

The Oregon & California reached Roseburg, on the South Umpqua, in 1872 and construction work halted there. A majority of the bonds of the railroad had been sold to German investors and when Holladay defaulted on the payments, the Teutons sent Henry Villard to Oregon in 1874 to salvage their investment.

Villard ousted Ben Holladay and installed Richard Koehler as resident manager. Koehler was a German railroader and could speak but little English, but he soon had the road producing revenue.

Under Villard's direction, grading was resumed south of Roseburg in the fall of 1881 and by 1884 the trains were running through Cow Creek Canyon and on to Grants Pass, thence up the Rogue River Valley to Ashland. The first train from Ashland to Portland was in charge of Conductor W. S. "Shan" Conser and Engineer Dennis McCarthy, with Jim Porter tossing the wood into the fire box of Engine 22.

Villard also pushed the west side road, forming the Western Oregon Railroad to build from St. Joseph to Corvallis, and this section was completed in 1880. He also built a short branch off the east side main line from Albany to Lebanon.

RAT HOLE. A brass-bound wood-burner of the Oregon & California Railroad stands at the east portal of Tunnel No. 1 in Cow Creek Canyon in this photo made May 17, 1883. Operations in this area were hampered by slides until the landscape settled, after having been disturbed by construction crews. (Courtesy of Southern Pacific)

OLD BETSY. Ben Holladay purchased this primitive engine from the portage railways at the Cascades to assist in construction of the Oregon Central Railroad in 1869. When the road became Oregon & California Railroad, the dinky was not numbered, but lettered "A." Boiler was of the return flue type, with stack passing smoke up through cab roof. (Courtesy of H. H. Arey)

FIRST PASSENGER TRAIN over Siskiyous from California to Oregon was pulled by this engine and crew on December 17, 1887. Left to right, Conductor George Morgan, Engineer Jack Clark, unknown, work train foreman Jack O'Neil, three unknown, assistant foreman Gus Loew, and unknown. Fireman in gangway is unidentified. (Courtesy of Siskiyou County Historical Society)

Control of the Oregon & California passed to the Southern Pacific in early 1887 and on December 17th, 1887, the line over the rugged Siskiyous was opened and the first train rolled in from California.

Henry Villard and a delegation of Oregon dignitaries prepared for a golden spike ceremony at Ashland to celebrate the arrival of the first California train. The affair was almost as much of a fiasco as Villard's Northern Pacific "last spike" ceremonies. The California delegation was due in Ashland around noon, but a work train was derailed in the Siskiyous and the special was delayed. The early dusk of winter fell on Ashland, along with a chill wind that toppled a big arch over the track bearing banners of welcome and evergreen decorations. Finally the bleary oil headlight of the special loomed around the curve, but it was so dark that a lantern had to be held while Col. Charles Crocker tapped home the golden spike.

Under Southern Pacific control, the O. & C. went through all of the growing pains accorded new roads in the Northwest. Cow Creek Canyon was the scene of numerous accidents and a couple of train robberies, one of which was foiled by the crew. When a huge slide blocked the canyon in 1890, the paymaster transferred his precious chests from the pay car into a wagon, hired a pair of rifle-toting natives for guards, and drove over the hills to pay off the crews working on the south end of the Portland Division.

The Southern Pacific added the Oregonian

BEARDED OLD "KING OF HURRY," the colorful Ben Holladay was a power in West Coast shipping, stage-coaching, and railroading. He built Ore. & Cal. R.R. from Portland to Roseburg before his transportation empire collapsed. (Courtesy of Oregon Historical Society)

READY TO ROLL. An Oregon & California "monkey hog," equipped with A. J. Stevens' valve gear, stands on the turntable at the Ashland roundhouse. The supply of two-foot wood, piled higher than the cab roof, had to be replenished several times on the 144-mile run north to Roseburg. (From a photo, courtesy of Oregon Historical Society)

ASHLAND ROUNDHOUSE serviced engines for the climb up the Siskiyous and for the run north to Roseburg.

MOVING DAY IN 1897. Wood-burner No. 31 of O.&C. carts old Grants Pass depot up over Louse Creek Summit to new location at Merlin. (Courtesy of John H. Young)

RELIEF TRAIN, powered by Ore. & Cal. R.R. Engine 39, hauls ties to Lake Labish after trestle there collapsed in 1890.

GEE UP, YOU LOP-EARED CUSSES! Spans of mules and one four-horse team pull scrapers to build railroad grade near Kirk, Oregon, 1925-26; track now used jointly by S.P. and G.N. Pile-driver works on bridge at left. (Courtesy of Southern Pacific)

NO TRAIN TODAY! Flooding South Yamhill River washed away part of bridge on West Side line in the late 1880's. (C. N. Bennett photo, courtesy Ralph Wortman)

DAMP TERMINAL of Oregon & California Railroad (Southern Pacific) at East Portland was a result of high water during the flood of 1890; peak of inundation came on February 5th. Behind depot at right, the O.R.&N. line circled Clinton's Point and headed east up Sullivan's Gulch.

JUNE FRESHET OF 1894 sent Willamette River out of its banks and flooded Portland railroad yards. Engines and cars marooned here stand in front of the Union Station. (Courtesy of Union Pacific R.R.)

NERVE CENTER OF RAILROAD, this is interior of train dispatcher's office around turn of the century at Roseburg, Oregon. Chief Dispatcher Ed Pengra, wearing derby, supervises work of "trick" dispatchers and operators; girl is Flossie Shambrook, clerk. (Courtesy of Grant Osborne)

"SALEM." Oregon & California Railroad No. 5 was one of road's named locomotives, built by Baldwin in 1870. Engineer Callicott made a record run from Salem to Portland with an engine of this type in 1872, rushing fire-fighting equipment to a blaze that destroyed over 20 blocks of the town's business district. (Courtesy of H. H. Arey)

OREGON & CALIFORNIA operated a fleet of these graceful 3-domed Baldwins. Engineer Bill Batman is seated in cab of No. 18, built in 1879.

FUNNEL STACK graced Oregon & California locomotive No. 21. This engine is reportedly the first to pull a passenger train in the Rogue River valley, 1884.

SPEED MERCHANT. S.P. 3068, an Atlantic with high drivers, was very fast. Crews called these "Shanghais."

"GRANTS PASS SPECIAL" of J. T. Flynn Co. hauled prospective land buyers over Ore. & Cal. R.R. in 1890. The two oil headlights on each locomotive enabled engine crews to watch for rocks and slides in Cow Creek Canyon.

OVERHEAD CATENARY fed juice to these fast West Side passenger units of Southern Pacific; locally called "Red Cars," they ran between Portland and Corvallis.

TRAIN TIME brings a bustle of activity to the Southern Pacific depot at Weed, California, as the second section of No. 16 arrives.

ROBBERY ON THE HIGH IRON. This express car of Southern Pacific's train No. 15 shows the effect of a dynamite explosion used by bandits to blow open the safe. The train was held up about 10:30 P.M. on March 31st, 1904, near Copley, Shasta County, California. Express messenger William J. O'Neill was killed during the hold-up.

SHASTA SPRINGS was a noted watering spot on railroad between Portland and San Francisco. Pair of wood-burners pause with "varnish" to allow passengers to sample the sparkling spring water in spring-house at right. (Courtesy of Southern Pacific)

AFTER A HARD DAY of bucking snow in the rugged Siskiyous in northern California, three Southern Pacific wood-burners take a break. (Courtesy of Southern Pacific)

DOWN IN THE CORNER, (reverse levers set to allow valves to receive steam during full stroke) three locomotives pound over curved Dollarhide Trestle as they boost a passenger train up the steep Siskiyou grade. Location is site of toll gate on old Dollarhide wagon road over mountains. (Courtesy of Southern Pacific)

UMPQUA TERMINAL. Oregon & California roundhouse at Roseburg was a busy place in the 1890's, nine wood-burning locomotives showing in this photo. Big 8-wheeler at far left, with straight stack, belonged to Astoria & Columbia River Railroad but was too heavy and was exchanged for a lighter O&C engine. These large locomotives were regarded as hoodoos by O&C crews because they frequently derailed; one overturned near Byers, killing Engineer Jimmy McCalley.

BAT CASEY'S PRIDE AND JOY. This is an interior view of the famous "nickleplated" locomotive, Fireman Fred Beard seated at left and Engineer Bartholomew "Bat" Casey at right, hand on the throttle. Note linoleum on floor, mirrors, mounted buck head, oil gauge lamp, and old "strong-arm" or manual reverse lever, called Johnson bar. Seth Thomas cab clock, upper right on gauge bracket, is in author's possession and still keeps accurate time. (Courtesy of Miss Helen Casey)

RIGHT HAND SIDE. View of the "throne" of a steam locomotive not long after the turn of the century, showing gauges and controls. Engineer straddling old-fashioned "Johnson bar" is Bill Lovett, veteran runner on the Southern Pacific's Portland Division. In the days of steam, engine crews roasted on one side and froze on the other.

BRASS HATS. Early view of Oregon & California R.R. enginehouse and shops at the station called Car Shops (now Brooklyn) in southeast Portland. Center figure on rear of private car is Division Supt. John Brandt, Jr.; his brother, A. Brandt, Master Mechanic, stands on walk platform at right. Others on car include Webb Ward, Yardmaster, and Washington, colored cook.

Railway and the Portland & Willamette Valley Railway to the Portland Division in the 1890's, converting these two roads to standard gauge. Around 1915, the Division was enlarged by the acquisition of the Corvallis & Eastern Railroad, the Pacific Railway & Navigation Company, the Salem, Falls City & Western Railroad, and a few minor short lines. A short time later, the subsidiary Willamette Pacific was completed to Coos Bay from Eugene, connecting with the Coos Bay, Roseburg & Eastern R.R. & Nav. Company, and both roads added to the Portland Division.

In 1926, the Natron Cut-off was opened, linking Eugene with Klamath Falls by a route over Willamette Pass in the Cascades; the pass was formerly called Pengra Pass, after a railroad surveyor. Two roads had been projected to connect Klamath Falls with the outside world by rail. The Oregon Midland Railroad was formed for this purpose in 1899, but only got as far as the survey stage. The Klamath Lake Railroad, primarily a logging line, started at Thrall, California, in 1901 and built a line to Pokegama, completed in 1903.

The Weed Lumber & Railroad Company finally built a road north from Weed that reached Klamath Falls in 1909, after coming under Southern Pacific control in 1906. This line was extended to Kirk and formed a link in the Natron Cut-off.

The original Oregon & California line through southwestern Oregon is still in service as a freight route, but all passenger trains from Portland to California use the new main line over the Cascades.

The fleet of graceful wood-burners that once ran through the fertile fields of the Willamette Valley gave way to newer oil-burners, and for years the Cascade Line trembled beneath the sixteen drivers of the huge articulated cab-in-front locomotives, uniquely Southern Pacific in design. These "back-up Mallies" were designed with their cabs foremost to give the engine crews better visibility and to put them ahead of the searing heat and gasses from the stacks, but even with this arrangement, the crews had to use respirators in the long tunnels.

Today, the colorful old steamers are gone and the Portland Division is dieselized. Powerful Diesel freight units growl up the "Big Hill" with their long trains, and sleek streamliners glide over the road where once the funnel-stacked, brass-bound Oregon & California locomotives spewed wood cinders on their brigades of wooden coaches, heading for glory and the dusty pages of history.

BALLOON STACK AND BAGPIPES
(O. Ry. Co.)

The village of Dayton, Oregon, drowses in the warmth of the autumn sunshine, a cluster of a few stores and shops embracing the shady town square. Tall firs tower over the old log blockhouse preserved in the park.

At the foot of the village, the narrow Yamhill River idles along, its calm surface broken occasionally by a rising bass.

Nothing is there to greet the eye of the casual visitor that would indicate life had not always been this serene. However, the scene was once one of great activity. Shallow draught sternwheelers once surged up to the grain chutes of the waterfront warehouses, and the whine of the sawmill at the mouth of Palmer Creek filled the air. When the broad fields of

UP FROM COW CREEK CANYON, Engine 31 of Ore. & Cal. R.R. stands with crew and old style side-door caboose at Glendale, Oregon. Bearded gent standing below cab window is "Pappy" Jamieson, pioneer conductor; portly man at far left is Mr. Guth, local saloon-keeper. (Courtesy of Mrs. Alfred Clarke)

LOCOMOTIVE ALBUM

MOVIE STAR. Old No. 4 of the Oregon & South Eastern began her railroad career on Colonel Hogg's Oregon Pacific line and was acquired by the O. & S. E. in 1902. Her blaze of glory came in 1926, when Buster Keaton starred in a comedy filmed along the Row River, east of Cottage Grove. The play was based on the Andrews raid during the Civil War. Old 4-Spot was chosen to play the role of the "**General**," the locomotive stolen by the Union raiders, and her wild dash delighted cinema fans on the flickering screens of the day. Mount Hood Railroad's original No. 1 played the role of "**Texas**" and was plunged through a burning trestle; her rusting remains lie in the Row River to this day.

ODD TANK ENGINE. Southern Pacific's No. 1901 was originally built for interurban service around the Oakland area in California by the Central Pacific in 1882. When the above photo was taken, she was running between Albany and Lebanon, Oregon. Veteran runner Bob McCalley stands in gangway. (Courtesy of Roderick A. McCalley)

WILLAMETTE VALLEY PASTORAL. Engine 20 of the Oregon & California Railroad was in freight service between Portland and Corvallis when this photo was made at Whiteson about 1890. Man at left is Conductor P. J. Gibson, next is Brakeman Ed Bodle. Others in crew are unidentified. Engine formerly ran on the line when it was known as the Western Oregon Railroad, was built by Baldwin in 1880, and later became S.P. 1512, then 1600, was sold to the Salem, Falls City & Western as their No. 7, returned to S.P. in 1915 and a year later was sold to the Oregon & South Eastern where she was again numbered 7.

SCHENECTADY PRODUCT, the 1959 was built in 1889 as No. 375 of the Southern Pacific. She later became Southern Pacific No. 2808, was sold to the Cananea, Rio Yaqui & Pacifico in 1906. This road, running from Nogales, Arizona, to Cananea, Sonora, Mexico, became part of the Southern Pacific of Mexico.

LONG AND FAITHFUL SERVICE. Old No. 2952 of the Southern Pacific was built by Schenectady in 1892 and rolled up many miles of hard use before being scrapped in 1951. Originally a cross compound, she was first numbered 2005, then 2852, and finally assigned to the 2900 series. She is shown here at Beaver Hill tank on the Coos Bay line, hauling logs out of Powers, shortly before her retirement.

THE "WENDLING BULLET" was the application hung on this mixed local serving the Wendling Branch of the Southern Pacific's lines in Oregon. Photo, taken in March, 1910, shows crew, left to right, Engineer Bob Gittens, Conductor Chas. Graham, Brakemen D. J. Bryan and Riley Snodgrass. Fireman Herb R. Rix leans from cab of Mogul type No. 1612. Note the "goose-egg" river rock used for ballast; it made very poor footing for the trainmen when switching. (Courtesy of H. R. Rix)

A Gallery of Steamers

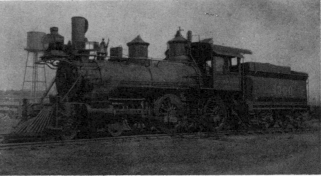

AMERICAN STANDARDS. The Oregon & California railroad, and its successor, the Southern Pacific, operated a fleet of trim 4-4-0 8-wheelers on the lines in Oregon. (No. 1) The O.&.C. 8 heads a passenger train at Myrtle Creek in the 1880's. (No. 2) No. 1203 of the S.P. was formerly O.&C. 4, built in 1870. (No. 3) No. 1248 was originally O.&C. 10, built in 1872. (No. 4) No. 1357, shown as a coal burner with extended front end at Ashland, was formerly O.&C. 24, built in 1883. (No. 5) No. 1300 was formerly No. 1 of the Corvallis & Eastern, built by Rogers in 1883. (No. 6) No. 1361 was formerly O.&C. No. 28, a Baldwin of 1883. (No. 7) No. 1358 was built for the O.&C. as their No. 25.
Credits: 1, 3, 4, and 7, D. L. Joslyn; 2, G. M. Best; 5 H. H. Arey.

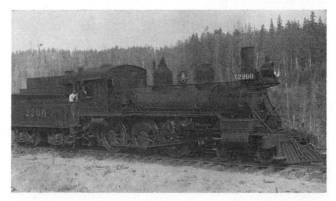

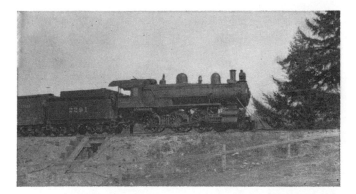

(No. 1) Engine 1254 was originally Ore. & Cal. R.R. 18, built in 1879.

(No. 2) The 1775, wooding up at Roseburg, was built as Central Pacific's 248 in 1888, later became Southern Pacific's 2204.

(No. 3) Originally Central Pacific's 2nd No. 175, this engine then became No. 1763 before being renumbered 2192.

(No. 4) Switcher 1021, built by Rhode Island in 1888, was scrapped in 1935. Note fire pump behind steam dome and hose reel on tank.

(No. 5) Built as Ore. & Cal. No. 45, this engine became S.P. 1908, then 2508, and was sold to the California & Oregon Coast R.R. where she was given the number 201, running out of Grants Pass.

(No. 6) No. 2200, a Stevens "monkey motion" 10-wheeler, was built in the Sacramento shops in 1888.

(No. 7) Southern Pacific's No. 2291 was a Vauclain compound built by Baldwin in 1902, later rebuilt simple. Scrapped in 1936.

THE VERSATILE TEN-WHEELER. Southern Pacific 4-6-0 types were put to many uses on the Portland Division. (No. 1) Engine 2223, with Engr. John Franzen, is shown at Portland's Union Station, ready for a passenger run. (No. 2) Engine 2085 handles a supply train, shown at Albany depot. (No. 3) Engines 2191 is shown at the smoky end of a freight train. (No. 4) Engine 2138 wears a pilot plow for bucking snow on the Tillamook line. (No. 5) Engine 2141 waits at Buxton to help Train 143 up the mountain to Timber. (No.'s 6 and 7) Engines 2001 and 2203 are shown in service on the Tillamook line. The 2001 is helping Mogul 1610 with a work train, while the 2203 displays indicators for Extra 2926, a freight run.

Yamhill County yielded their golden harvest, a line of teams and wagons nearly a mile long awaited their turn to unload the fat sacks of grain for shipment down-river.

The farmers and tradesmen of Yamhill County were not satisfied with the monopoly of the Oregon Central, and in the fall of 1877, they organized the Dayton, Sheridan & Grand Ronde Railroad and proposed to construct a road about 20 miles long, from the steamer landing at Dayton up to Sheridan. In the interest of lower construction costs, a narrow-gauge of 3 feet was selected.

The stock was soon subscribed and many of the farmers took their shares in the form of transportation script.

When May's blossoms were perfuming the warm breezes, 140 Chinamen trudged up from the Dayton landing and soon the dark earth of new grading traced a line across the green fields. President B. B. Branson, his board of directors, and promoter Joseph Gaston bustled about the countryside, and soon the citizens of Dallas, in neighboring Polk County, voted a subsidy to induce the little road to build a branch into their city.

Early in July of 1878, the big ocean side-wheeler, "GREAT REPUBLIC," steamed into Portland with enough rails for 10 miles of slim-gauge track stowed in her hold, and shortly after, the sternwheeler "S. T. CHURCH" paddled up to Dayton with a 40-ton load of iron.

SHETLAND PONY VERSION OF IRON HORSE, this 3-foot gauge locomotive was running on farmer-built Dayton, Sheridan & Grand Ronde R.R. when photo was taken at Dayton, Oregon, in 1878. Engine is No. 1, "PIONEER," or No. 2, "PROGRESS"; both were 2-4-0 type built by W. H. Bailey back in Connellsville, Pennsylvania, and weighed slightly over 10 tons each.

Hand-hewn fir ties had been strung along the new grade at Dayton, and G. B. Abdill was soon busy, hauling the rails from the boat landing up to the right of way with his yoke of oxen. The grading was soon completed between Dayton and Sherdian, and the Chinese were spiking down some 2 miles of track a week. In addition to the rails, car castings came up-river and a force of workmen started construction of the first rolling stock.

DEPARTED GLORY. Busy terminal at Dayton, on the Yamhill River, with sawmill, steamboats, warehouses, and tiny engine of the Dayton, Sheridan & Grand Ronde Railroad as they appeared about 1878.

SLIM PRINCESS. Engine 5 of the Oregonian Railway was polished to a high gloss when this photo was taken in 1888; building in rear is the old Whiteson hotel. Crew, left to right, include Brakeman Chas. Young, Fireman Ellis, Engr. Chas. Mahoney, and Brakeman Lou Keyser. The crosshead cold water pump for supplying the boiler can be plainly seen. (C. N. Bennett photo, courtesy Ralph Wortman)

When Captain James Carroll piloted the "GREAT REPUBLIC" north from San Francisco in mid-July, there was great rejoicing for her cargo included the first locomotive for the road. This little iron colt was built by W. H. Bailey of the National Locomotive Works in Connellsville, Pennsylvania. She was of the 2-4-0 wheel arrangement, with 31-inch drivers, and tipped the scales at 21,200 pounds. Proudly emblazoned on her cab panels was her name, "PIONEER."

The sternwheeler, "McMINNVILLE," bore the little 1-Spot up to Dayton. Temporary tracks had been laid down the steep incline at the old ferry landing, but the climb was too much for the "PIONEER" and her four tiny drivers spun futilely as she tried to climb up the bank.

The resourceful farmer-railroaders came quickly to her rescue. A stump puller was set up at the top of the incline and a cable fastened to the locomotive. A team of mules, the property of W. T. Hash, trotted around the sweep, the cable tightened, and the engine rolled up the steep pitch and off onto the level track of the main line.

With Engineer William Anderson at the throttle, the dinky was soon hard at work, transporting rails to the end of track.

August saw the arrival of Engine No. 2, a twin sister of the "PIONEER." This second locomotive was aptly named, "PROGRESS."

The road was completed to Sheridan and the first train ran up from Dayton on October 24th, 1878, loaded down with all the townsfolk who could find a place to perch. It was a great day for the narrow-gauge, but dark clouds were in the offing.

Money in the treasury dwindled away and debts piled up. Business was good, but most of it was being paid for with the transportation script and actual cash was not available.

George Revette was appointed receiver in early 1879, and soon after Mr. William Reid, representing Scottish interests, satisfied the debts and reorganized the road as the Willamette Valley Railway Company.

The Willamette Valley Railway was reorganized in 1880, emerging as the Oregon Railway Company, and later in the year the firm was changed to the Oregonian Railway Company, Ltd., with headquarters in Dundee, Scotland.

With the influx of Scotch money, the little line came to life with a boom. The Dallas branch, completed earlier, was extended south to Airlie, in Kings Valley. A cut-off near Dayton carried the rails north to Aiken, which was at once renamed Dundee, in honor of the Scottish city. Headquarters for the operation of the road were set up at Dundee, and shops were moved there from Dayton. Plans were started for a bridge across the Willamette and construction was started on the East Side Division in April, 1880, when ground was broken at Silverton.

A crowd of 1,200 gathered in the Silverton park to witness the ceremonies. American and Scotch flags were unfurled, the band tootled, and the wife of Governor W. W. Thayer turned the first spade of earth. From Silverton, the line was built west to Ray's Landing on the Willamette, and the ferry "MARGIE" ran across the river to Fullquartz's Landing, where the branch from Dundee dipped down to the west shore. From Silverton, work was pushed on the extension south. This line led over Macleay hill, and was completed to Coburg in July, 1882, passing through Brownsville and Scio.

President Reid ordered 4 new Mogul type locomotives, 65 new freight cars, and 7 passenger coaches. The new engines were fine little machines, weighing about 36,000 pounds, and were all wood-burners built by H. K. Porter.

More equipment was needed and 21 flat cars were built in Seattle and shipped down to Kalama, where the "CITY OF SALEM" took them up to the Scotch road. Warehouses were erected all along the line to care for the bumper wheat crop of 1880.

In the fall of 1880, the nobleman who headed the Scotch firm paid a visit to Oregon to view the properties. He was David Graham Drummond Ogilvie, Earl of Airlie. He was greatly impressed with Reid's progress and ordered construction of the proposed bridge over the Willamette, as well as surveys over the Cascades, the latter with the view of extending the line southeast toward a connection with the Central Pacific.

Three ocean vessels, the "CHILDERS," "SAN LUIS," and "NORTH BEND," were under charter to carry new rails from Cardiff and Middleboro-on-Tees. The new steel rails were a far cry from the 28-pound iron on the original Dayton-Sheridan line. This old rail had the nerve-wracking habit of breaking loose at the web and creating "snake-heads," long iron splinters that curled under the weight of passing trains and sometimes penetrated the car floors.

The slim-gauge trains clattered up and down both sides of the Willamette Valley, guided by such engineers as Sam Scanlon, Ed Ford, and Johnny Palmer. Trainmen included Conductors John Poorman, Joel Crocker and Brakemen Tom Feeney, Jim Porter, Lou Keyser, Charley Young, and Cyrus N. Bennett. For a time, a native son of Silverton fired for Johnny Palmer. This lad was later to achieve widespread fame as a cartoonist, the prominent Homer Davenport. A drawing of his dog, Duffy, long adorned the inner wall of the Silverton freight house.

Henry Villard, controlling the Oregon & California Railroad, was worried by the threat of the narrow-gauge extensions over the Cascades and a proposed extension to Yaquina and Astoria, so he took steps to end the menace. The

"C. N. SCOTT" was 3-foot gauge Oregonian Railway's No. 8 and bore the name of road's receiver. Engineer John Palmer is seated in cab in this photo made on the East Side Division of the line.

IRON COLT shown here is the Oregonian Railway's No. 7, pulling her two-car passenger train into Dallas in 1880. Engineer Sam Scanlon is seated with his hand on the throttle of the 3-foot gauge H. K. Porter Loco. Works product. Train is reputed to be the first to enter Dallas, which won Polk County seat away from river town of Independence on strength of having railroad service.

shrewd old German sent General J. B. Montgomery to Scotland and negotiated a long-term lease of the Oregonian properties, for his Oregon Ry. & Nav. Company.

As soon as Villard took control, (in August, 1881), he ordered all construction stopped and turned the road into a series of feeder lines for his Oregon & California Railroad. Portions of the system were abandoned, and after Villard left the control of the O.R.&N. in 1884, that concern repudiated the lease and the ruins of

GANDY DANCERS. Track gang prepares to widen 3-foot gauge track of Oregonian Railway to standard gauge after Southern Pacific had acquired the line in the 1890's. Rails were laid without tie plates and weight of passing trains soon caused them to cut into soft fir ties. (Courtesy of Ralph Wortman)

the road were handed over to Receiver Charles N. Scott.

Receiver Scott borrowed funds and began the task of putting the road back into profitable operation. New ties were laid, and gravel ballast raised the track out of the mud. In connection with Scott's program, William Reid formed the Portland & Willamette Valley Railway to complete the abandoned line from Dundee to Portland. Work was started in 1886 and the road was completed onto the Jefferson Street levee in Portland in July, 1888.

Reid obtained 3 locomotives for the P.&W.V., all of them of the 2-6-0 type. Number 1 was a Baldwin built for the Utah & Northern, while the 2 and 3 were New York Loco. Works products, formerly used on the Cincinnati Northern.

In spite of the terrible conditions of the track, the road suffered surprisingly few accidents. Derailments were frequent, but the slow speed made these more annoying than dangerous. One fatality did occur when a fir tree toppled through the timbers of Deadman's Trestle on the Dundee-Oswego line. A train descending the grade plunged through the gaping break,

JERRY, GO ILE THE CAR . . . so ran the poem about the old Irish section foreman. Here is a typical section gang with their hand-pumper in 1888, Frank Gould's crew, ready for a day of tamping ties or changing out rail; depot is at Sheridan, on Oregonian Ry.'s 3-foot line.

and Fireman Johnny Hohenlightner was crushed to death in his shattered cab.

The bridge over the Willamette was never built, and the cars from the East Side Division were ferried across at Ray's Landing to the Dundee connection. The banks of the river are steep at Ray's Landing and a locomotive once failed to stop in time, plunging up to her stack in the river. She was hauled out, wet and muddy, but undamaged by her unexpected baptism.

In 1890, the Southern Pacific Company foreclosed the Oregonian Railway, and obtained the Portland & Willamette Valley Railway in 1892. Again portions of the line were abandoned, and the remainder was soon converted to standard gauge and passed into the Espee's Portland Division.

The trim little engines were scattered to various slim-gauge pikes up and down the Pacific Coast, some to roads in California and one to the Ilwaco road in Washington. So carelessly were records kept in those boisterous times that no one knows what disposition was made of the "PIONEER" and the "PROGRESS," nor of Engines 3 and 5. Indeed, no record exists at all of Engine No. 3, if the road ever had such a locomotive.

The roster of engines on the road ended with

No. 8, a Baldwin 8-wheeler named the "C. N. SCOTT." In his declining years, the veteran Cy Bennett recalled the remains of a small engine had lain rusting in the weeds at Ray's Landing during his time on the road, and thought she might have been a home-made affair used in building the East Side Division . . . perhaps this was the derelict 3-Spot.

The steamboats no longer plow the winding Yamhill, and only a scattered few old settlers

BLACKSMITH SHOPS of narrow-gauge Oregonian Ry. at Dundee, Oregon, about 1881. Crew hand-forged all frogs used on line in this crude shop from ordinary sections of rail, also repaired rolling stock.

WOODEN DRAWBRIDGE over the Willamette River at Albany, Oregon, was reputed to be the longest of its type in the world when completed in 1887. Oregon Pacific Railroad passenger train is arriving from Yaquina while stern-wheeler believed to be the "MODOC" loads cargo at the Red Crown Mills.

TYPICAL CONSTRUCTION CAMP, tent houses cooking facilities and mess tables. One-horse dump cart above is on grade of Oregon Pacific Railroad, pushing toward Hogg Pass in high Cascades. (Courtesy of Oregon State Archives)

AFTER CONVERSION from narrow gauge, the Oregonian Ry. was operated as a standard gauge road for some time before being absorbed into the Southern Pacific. This is Engine 11 with a train at Dallas. Veteran conductor Joel Crocker stands by pilot of Rogers-built eight-wheeler, Fireman "Dode" Goyeau is in gangway.

can recall the rambling 180-mile Oregonian Railway. The picturesque little road has vanished, leaving only a fragrant memory.

COLONEL HOGG'S DREAM
(WV&CRR-O.P.RR)

The coast line of Oregon is indented with numerous bays and harbours, most of them watered by the streams that flow down from the timbered watersheds of the Coast Range. Where the fresh waters meet the salt flood, the tidelands are alternately submerged or exposed to reek in the sun. Gulls wheel and cry over the drift, and the marsh grass bends before the tangy breeze.

Such an estuary is Yaquina Bay, watered by the twisting river of the same name.

Early settlers around the bay region came in by boat or over the Indian and game trails, but by 1871 a toll road for wagons had been hacked out from Yaquina Bay's up-river port of Elk City to Corvallis.

The year 1871 also saw the arrival of Colonel T. E. Hogg, a railroad promoter who was destined to flash his star over the transportation fields of western Oregon, only to see it fall to earth in cold ashes. The Colonel was a Democrat and his fortune and business had been swept away with the fall of the Confederacy. Whatever defeats shadowed his past, the

Colonel cast them off and promptly set about to organize a railroad to build from the Willamette Valley to Yaquina Bay. His first concern was the Corvallis & Yaquina Bay Railroad Company, set up in 1872. This was followed by a new corporation, the Willamette Valley & Coast Railroad, organized in 1874.

The citizens of Benton County rallied behind the Colonel and some grading was done on a line west of Corvallis toward Philomath, starting in 1877.

In a search for capital to complete his road, the ex-rebel turned to the money markets of Europe, and in 1877 he put in an appearance in

TIME OUT FOR "BEANS." Oregonian Railway's narrow-gauge 7-Spot stands in front of Mary Stone's house near Dallas, a favored eating place for crews in early 1880's. Crew include Fireman Sam Scanlon in gangway, Engineer Ed Ford in cab, Brakeman C. N. Bennett by cylinder, Conductor Gould or Fuller standing on pilot. Man seated on pilot is red-bearded Mike Rielly, car repairer; Dallas station agent lolls on cab roof.

LITTLE "CORVALLIS" was first locomotive of the Willamette Valley & Coast Railroad. Engine was built by the Grant Locomotive Works in 1874, and used in construction of line between Corvallis and Yaquina. Note the set of deer horns mounted on headlight. (Courtesy of H. H. Arey)

England. Here he fell in with Wallis Nash, who arranged an audience with prospective investors. The Colonel extolled the unlimited opportunities, and backing his testimony was the gaunt old greybeard, Sir James Douglas, formerly Governor of the Hudson's Bay Company, who was familiar with the great natural resources of the Northwest.

Stirred by the reports of these two, Wallis Nash came to Oregon in 1877, to personally inspect the proposed route and the agricultural possibilities of the country. Nash was greatly impressed by what he saw, and upon his return to England wrote and published a book dealing with the region.

In the spring of 1879, Nash set sail from Liverpool for Oregon, bringing along his sick wife, one son, and four young Englishmen, students on the remittance plan.

In 1880, Colonel Hogg formed the Oregon Pacific Railroad, to finance the operations of his Willamette Valley & Coast R.R., and Nash was elected second vice president. The first vice president was William M. Hoag, a brother of Colonel Hogg. Not only did the brothers differ in the spelling of the family name, they were opposed in political belief as well. Colonel Hogg was the dreamer of grandiose dreams, while "Uncle Billy" Hoag, as he became known to the crews, was the practical doer of deeds.

Grading was carried on from both the Corvallis and Yaquina ends of the road, and the road's first locomotive, a small 2-4-0 built by the Grant Works and named "CORVALLIS," was shipped back and forth to aid in the work.

It was not until March of 1885 that the first through train puffed and panted over the Coast Range between the two terminals.

The first excursion train over the road was slated to leave Corvallis on July 4th, 1885, and consisted of a string of flatcars fitted out with benches. The little "CORVALLIS" struggled up to Summit and halted near the entrance to one of the road's three tunnels. The timbering in this "rat-hole" had been destroyed by fire a short time before, and the crowd walked around to the western end, where one of the new eight-wheelers from the Yaquina end was waiting with more flatcars.

The excursionists were rolled into Yaquina in grand style, but when the return trip started on July 6th, all was not so merry. The weather had turned extremely hot, causing the new track to buckle in many places from "sun kinks" caused by the expansion of the rails. It was late afternoon by the time the wilted vacationers reached the blockaded tunnel and trudged over the ridge to load up behind the "CORVALLIS." The tiny engine chuffed bravely up and into the tunnel nearest the summit, but the combination of a heavy train and slimy rails inside the bore was too much for her and she stalled, slipping down in a shower of soot and wood cinders. Muddy water dripped down on the bedraggled passengers, exposed on their open cars, and the tea-kettle was forced to back out and make a second run before she panted through and clanked on down the Mary's River canyon and into Corvallis. This excursion was only the forerunner of many to follow. Since Corvallis was "dry" by local option, crowds flocked to Yaquina and ferried down the bay to "wet" Newport. So heavy was this bar-bound traffic that hangovers in Corvallis were dubbed "train sickness."

Colonel Hogg, however, had greater plans for his road than for it to become a jitney service for saloon patrons. The map hanging in the Corvallis office had a heavy line traced across it, leading east through Albany, up the north fork of the Santiam River, and out across the high desert of eastern Oregon to Boise, Idaho. The tracing indicated the proposed extension that the Colonel envisioned, crossing the summit of the Cascades by an easy grade leading through the gap that was later named Hogg Pass. At Boise, or some indefinite point near the Idaho border, the new railroad would connect with the Oregon Short Line, or, better still, with a rumored westward transcontinental connection to be built by the Chicago & Northwestern.

Three fine sternwheelers were placed on the run from Corvallis to Portland, doing a good local and through trade along the Willamette River. These boats were the "WILLIAM M.

HOAG," "THREE SISTERS," and "N. S. BENT-LEY."

From Yaquina Bay, the water lines operated a coastal steamer service south to San Francisco. The first of these ocean vessels was the "YAQUINA CITY," placed on the route in September, 1885. This vessel was lost inside Yaquina Bar in December, 1887. The loss was termed an accident, and the wrecked steamer was replaced in 1888 by the "YAQUINA BAY," formerly the "CARACAS." On her first trip she grounded near Yaquina's south jetty and broke up. Now the local tongues began to wag and it was darkly hinted that the wrecking of both vessels was deliberate sabotage by hostile interests. Other ocean vessels were used on the route, and the tugs "RESOLUTE" and "FAVORITE" plodded around Yaquina Bay.

The eastward extension from Corvallis to Albany was opened for service in early 1887,

IN THE WILDS OF WESTERN OREGON, construction gang loads work train at a rail storage depot on the Willamette Valley & Coast R.R. Note the hand-hewn ties used by early railroad builders, often cut from dense stands of timber along right of way.

following the autumn visit in 1886 of a group of Eastern capitalists including John Blair and Percy R. Pyne. These gentlemen were not only bondholders of the Oregon Pacific, but directors of the Chicago & Northwestern as well.

Business boomed on the road and to handle the increasing rail traffic, a fleet of graceful locomotives was added to the roster. Mostly 8-wheelers, they were built by the Cooke Locomotive Works and by the Rogers Locomotive Works. In all, the road eventually owned 16 engines. These iron horses were all standard gauge wood-burners, and were kept shined, polished, and in good mechanical repair.

The ribbons of steel crept east from Albany and up the canyon of the North Santiam. High in Hogg Pass, a short length of track was laid to hold the right of way over the summit, and running gear, packed laboriously into the wilderness, was set upon it and a boxcar constructed. This car was rolled over the track by mule or horse power to establish the Hogg claim of prior rights to the location. Far off in the eastern reaches of the state, an Oregon Pacific gang graded a stretch of roadbed in the rough Malheur River canyon for similar purposes.

Troubles arose between contractors Geo. W. Hunt and Nelson Bennett and the railroad company in 1887, and new contracts were let in 1888. The line passed east through the hamlet of Mill City and on up through Detroit station, but came to a dismal halt at Boulder Creek, 12 miles short of the Cascade summit.

Money problems became so acute in 1890 that the line was placed in receivership. The road fell into disrepair and the wages lagged as much as 10 months in arrears. The property was sold and resold by the Benton County sheriff, and a succession of receivers tried to operate the line, but the efforts failed. In 1894, A. B. Hammond and associates bought the road at a sheriff's sale for $100,000. This was perhaps one of the greatest railroad bargains of all time. The new company, organized as the Oregon Central & Eastern Railway, received about 143 miles of railroad, including 13,300 tons of good English steel rail of Sheffield and other manufacture, 16 locomotives, 258 box cars, the ocean steamship "WILLAMETTE VALLEY," the bar tug "RESOLUTE," the three river steamboats, passenger coaches, machine shop tools, depots, roundhouses, and all other appurtenances. The

TIME OUT FOR FUEL. Willamette Valley & Coast 3-Spot at wood pile in 1880's; cutting two-foot wood for railroad was source of income for settlers along line. (Moorhouse photo, Oregon Collection, University of Ore.)

previous receiver had set a conservative scrap value on the properties at $374,700.

In 1897, Hammond incorporated the Corvallis & Eastern Railroad to succeed the Oregon Central & Eastern. The floating equipment and some of the rolling stock was sold by Hammond for a sum that Wallis Nash estimated at $192,-000, or $92,000 more than he had paid for the entire layout. In 1907 he sold the Corvallis & Eastern to Edward H. Harriman for a reported $750,000, a tidy profit on the original $100,000 investment.

The road was absorbed into the Portland Division of the Harriman-controlled Southern Pacific Lines, and portions of it today constitute the Toledo and the Mill City branches of that road. Wallis Nash attempted to complete the extension east in 1906, organizing the Mid-Oregon & Eastern Railway, but the project died in the paper stages.

Thus ended the dream of Colonel T. E. Hogg. The great overland system of his dreams never materialized, but the old Rebel was a fighter to the last ditch. His project had merit and he was still waging a battle to regain control when he was struck down by apoplexy aboard a Philadelphia street car in 1896.

The motive power of the original road was scattered far and wide after A. B. Hammond took control. Several of the engines were shipped off to Hammond's Astoria & Columbia River Railroad, later passing to the Spokane, Portland & Seattle Railway. One of the 8-wheelers went north to the Tacoma & Eastern, another pair to the Oregon & South Eastern, and

EIGHT-STALL ROUNDHOUSE of Oregon Pacific Railroad at Albany was built in 1887 with brick made by convict labor in San Quentin prison. The car on blocks at the left is a caboose being constructed by road's shop forces.

GRAVE CREEK BRIDGE carried the Oregon & California tracks over this deep canyon during construction in 1884. Engine pulling train load of ties and material is manned by Engr. D. McCarthy and Fireman James Porter. (Courtesy of Southern Oregon Historical Society)

CALIFORNIA & OREGON COAST RAILROAD No. 1 was built by Rogers in 1872 as the Central Pacific's 180, later passed to the Southern Pacific and was sold to the Grants Pass & Eastern as their No. 1 in 1911. Road ran from Grants Pass to Waters Creek and was torn up in recent years, after being owned municipally by Grants Pass.

CENTRAL PACIFIC'S "ONEONTA" stands at wood-pile at Cisco, California, in days when first transcontinental line was being built; stacks of rail in foreground and construction material at warehouses in rear being loaded into freight wagons indicate supply depot. (Courtesy of Southern Pacific)

OREGON & CALIFORNIA RAILROAD'S No. 22 was handling the only passenger train running out of Ashland when this picture was taken there about 1884. Men include Agent Kane, at left, Conductor Tom Kearney, standing by cross-head, and Fireman Jim Porter, holding long spouted oil can. (Courtesy of Southern Oregon Historical Society)

CHECKMATE. Corvallis & Eastern Eng. 6 blocks efforts of Oregon Electric to cross C&E line in Albany, Ore. O.E. grade can be seen on both sides of engine "holding the fort." (Courtesy Southern Pacific)

two more were sold south, one to the Yreka Railroad and another to the Oregon & Eureka. The Rogue River Valley Railroad bought Cooke-built No. 5, a small 2-4-0 type. No record exists on the disposal of the dainty little "CORVALLIS," the pioneer locomotive on the road.

Today, the powerful Diesels of the Southern Pacific growl over the steep climb to Summit, the crest of the Coast Range. The smoke from the balloon-stacked wood-eaters has long ago faded, but perhaps their rusty ghosts still clatter silently through the night, when the fog hangs over Yaquina and the trails of misty vapor drift through the rain forest, eddying in the sea breeze that wafts inland from the Pacific.

"THE HIGH-WHEELED TWO" was a favorite with early crews on the old Willamette Valley & Coast Railroad; she was a fast-stepping product of the Rogers Locomotive Works. Local wags dubbed the road the "Wet Valley & Constant Rainy Region" from its initials and the heavy precipitation along its route.

UP THE SANTIAM CANYON, Oregon Pacific's No. 10 and crew pose near the end of the eastward Cascade extension. Hand-hewn ties support rails over a pole culvert. One-armed mountaineer and his dogs have come down to look over the new-fangled "iron horse."

ELEGANCE IN THE EIGHTIES. Willamette Valley & Coast Railroad passenger train is headed by No. 6, a shiny Cooke eight-wheeler. Coaches were equipped with new Miller "hook" coupler, came second-hand from the Rochester, Hornellsville & Lackawanna in far-off New York State. Conductor Kennedy and Engineer Ford stand at left in photo.

WATCHING THE TRAIN COME IN was a favorite pastime of village idlers and small boys, many of the latter aspiring to become railroad men. Group gathered here stands in front of Toledo depot while C.&E. No. 7 pauses with a 4-car mixed train.

CLOTHING SMEARED WITH GREASE has long been the trade-mark of railroad shop forces. Machinists, boiler-makers, and other employees of the Albany roundhouse pose here on Corvallis & Eastern No. 5, spotted on the old wooden "gallows" type turntable. (Courtesy of H. H. Arey)

WOODING UP was a never-ending chore as hungry fire-boxes rapidly consumed fuel. Corvallis & Eastern brake-men have shucked their uniform coats to join fireman in pitching 2-foot lengths of fir onto tender of old 2-Spot.

VALLEY BOUND. C.&E. log train at the cribbing along the Santiam River, with coach at rear for passengers.

GOOD OLD DAYS. Corvallis & Eastern Engine 3 standing at Summit depot. Men, left to right, included Brakeman George Woods, Condr. Elmer Daniels, Fireman Frank Blodgett, Brakeman Walter Winkler (holding what suspiciously looks like a bottle of "liquid cheer"), the two Nash brothers (Sons of Vice President Wallis Nash), and the station agent, who may be R. K. Montgomery. Rule G, forbidding strong drink, was largely ignored on the old Yaquina line.

KNEE-DEEP IN SNOW, the Corvallis & Eastern 9-Spot sizzles in front of the Cascade Hotel at Detroit, Oregon. (Courtesy of H. H. Arey)

THE OLD GOAT. Oregon & California R.R. No. 43 was an 0-4-0 switch engine, the only one of its kind on the road. Built by Baldwin in 1883, she later became S.P.'s 1011, and was sold to the short-line Independence & Monmouth Railroad in 1905. (Courtesy of D. L. Joslyn)

OREGON & CALIFORNIA R.R. No. 45 was one of the "monkey-motion" 2-8-0 types built in the Sacramento shops in 1887. (Courtesy of D. L. Joslyn)

CAPITOL CITY SHUNTER. Oregon & California No. 1244 does a bit of station switching in front of the wooden depot at Salem, Oregon, around 1890. (Courtesy of Helen Casey)

LINK AND PIN LINE-UP. Four Southern Pacific engines stand outside the Roseburg, Oregon, roundhouse in the good old days. At the left, badly battered in a wreck, is 10-wheeler 1768; next are the 1355 and 1543, a brace of 8-wheelers; last is No. 1773, another 10-wheeler.

PIONEER VARNISH. Oregon & California Eng. 3 and a passenger train at New Era, on Portland Div. main line.

HAND-POWERED WRECKING CRANE struggles to clear debris from wreck at Tunnel No. 1 after bridge collapsed on April 29, 1895. Oregon Pacific Railroad was in receivership at the time and was operating as the Oregon Central & Eastern R.R. Insets show Conductor Campbell and Brakeman Wilcox, both killed when cars on which they were setting hand brakes plunged into Yaquina River. (From a Crawford & Paxton photo)

NARROW ESCAPE was had by passengers of this Corvallis & Eastern train when it was derailed near Chitwood, Oregon, in November, 1912.

LOOK PRETTY, BOYS. Train and engine crew of Corvallis & Eastern mixed job drape over and around pilot of Engine No. 2 shortly after the turn of the century to have their picture taken.

"RAILS" OF THE OLD SCHOOL. Crew on Oregon Pacific got together to pose for this studio photo. Seated, left to right, are Baggageman Walter Bargess, Brakeman Al Wall, and Express Messenger Bill Toner; standing at left is Engineer Ed Ford, formerly a runner on Oregonian Ry. and later on Astoria & Columbia River R.R., while gent with magnificent moustache is Conductor Charlie Kennedy.

STEEL AT TIDEWATER is depicted in this view of Willamette Valley & Coast R.R. terminus at Yaquina, on bay of same name. Crew is turning Engine No. 7 on old "arm-strong" turntable while other engines occupy stalls in wooden roundhouse. Ocean vessel at dock at western end of rail yards made connections for San Francisco. Barge moored behind locomotive housed a floating saloon, flouting local option that forbid the sale of strong drink; location chosen by One-legged Jack, the owner, was an ideal one as early crews needed fortification to battle steep Coast Range grades with primitive equipment.

PREFABRICATING BRIDGE TIMBERS, carpenters of Willamette Valley & Coast R.R. wield saw and adze while Engine No. 11 stands with construction train in background. (From a Crawford & Paxton photo)

Frozen North

GOLD RUSH ROUTE
(WP&Y.)

When the steamer "PORTLAND" warped in alongside the Schwabacher Wharf in the Puget Sound metropolis of Seattle in 1897 her famous "Ton of Gold" cargo touched off the great Klondike mining excitement. Swarms of depression-wearied men from all walks of life fought for passage to the new El Dorado. Every ancient tub that could float deposited scores of prospectors at Dyea and Skagway, Alaska, at the head of the Lynn Canal.

Ahead of these Argonauts of the Far North lay two equally heartbreaking ways to the golden riches of Dawson and the Klondike. These two trails led over Chilkoot Pass and White Pass, great snowy barriers that dwarfed the ant-like line of weary miners who struggled up the icy, nearly-perpendicular slopes.

To overcome this difficult and hazardous journey, the White Pass Railway was organized and construction begun at Skagway in 1898.

The route selected into the Klondike was 110 miles in length. To lessen construction costs, the narrow gauge of 3 feet was chosen for the width of track.

British capital financed the road, headed by the firm of Close Brothers, and E. C. Hawkins was engaged as Chief Engineer.

The contractor building the line out of Skagway was Michael J. Heney, with P. J. O'Brien as bridge constructor. By July 2, 1898, Mike Heney had the first mile of track laid and the first locomotive in Alaska running upon it. The engine was a diamond-stacker built by the Baldwin Locomotive Works and was a 2-6-0, or Mogul, type.

After the first 5 miles of track were spiked down the road began to encounter difficult going. Almost constant rockwork was necessary to push the rails up to White Pass summit. From sea level at Skagway the line climbed to an elevation of 2,885 feet in just over 20 miles. The roadbed had to be hacked and blasted out of the sheer rock walls and 2,000 men were em-

PARKAS, MITTENS, AND MUKLUKS. White Pass & Yukon railroaders and their ladies with the first passenger train at the summit of White Pass, February 20. 1899. E. A. Hegg photo, courtesy of Joe Williamson.

ployed in the task. The labor turnover was high because of the extreme hardships of the job during the winter months. Weary laborers threw down their tools and hiked back to the glowing lights of Skagway.

The blasting caused great avalanches of snow to engulf the new grade and rock slides also hampered construction.

The track reached the summit of White Pass on February 20, 1899, and a celebration was held in Mike Heney's tent. However, a new obstacle appeared at the summit in the form of a British guard. The boundary question between Alaska and British Columbia at this location had not been settled and the guard was posted to prevent the track from crossing into British territory. Rumors filtered down to Skagway that Mike Heney had dispatched a local character called "Stikine Bill" up to pay the guard a social visit, armed with two bottles of Scotch whisky and a box of cigars. When the glorious hangover ended the two ribbons of steel were across the disputed border and winding down toward the shores of Lake Bennett.

On July 6, 1899, the line was completed to Bennett, a distance of 40 miles from Skagway, and an excursion train came out to the end of track. The locomotive was decorated with Canadian and American flags; the crowd of excursionists rode on open flat cars. On the return trip to Skagway this first train carried back $500,000 in gold dust!

Meanwhile, construction was being pushed from the Whitehorse end of the line and the rails were joined at Caribou Crossing on July 29, 1900. The name of the station was later shortened to Carcross.

The road had cost about $2,000,000 to build but the traffic was heavy and in 1904, after the first pressure of the Klondike rush had slackened, the rail and river operations netted over $700,000. In that year the road boasted a roster of 16 locomotives, 13 passenger cars, 257 freight cars, and four cabooses. The freight equipment included box cars, stock cars, coal gondolas, flat cars, and even 4 refrigerator cars. Nineteen steamboats plied the Yukon.

The fortunes of the line rose and fell until the outbreak of World War II when the United States leased the road to aid in our Arctic de-

YUKON GATEWAY, this spectacular view shows a White Pass & Yukon mixed train in the rugged mountains pierced by the narrow gauge line. Parlor cars are named for lakes in the region served by the W. P. & Y. (Courtesy of White Pass & Yukon Route)

EAST FORK OF SKAGWAY RIVER was crossed by White Pass & Yukon on timber trestle. Engine is shown here with the first passenger train over the road. E. A. Hegg photo, courtesy of Joe Williamson.

fense problems. Vast amounts of material were needed for a pipe line and for the White Horse Air Base and the equipment and personnel of the WP&Y required assistance to move it.

To assist the civilian personnel in operating the road two detachments of U.S. troops were shipped north. These men were from the 713th and 727th Railway Operating Battalions and were used as the nucleus of the new 770th Ry. Opr. Bn.; Colonel W. P. Wilson, an experienced

IRON HORSE on the Trail of '98 is this Baldwin Mogul of the White Pass & Yukon, posed here with her proud crew at Skagway in 1900. Steam sizzles from her safety valve, an indication that the fireman lolling in the gangway has the boiler hot and "loaded" for the steep climb to summit of White Pass.

narrow-gage operating Superintendent from the Colorado & Southern Ry., was placed in command.

Severe weather caused a blockade of the road for 10 days in February of 1943. The temperature dropped to 30° below and stayed there, while driving winds piled huge drifts over the steel trail on White Pass. The civilian and military crews finally managed to reopen the line by heroic efforts, even burning ties in the locomotives when the coal supply was exhausted. The White Pass & Yukon owned two rotary snowplows and the Army added a third one to help combat the blizzards. The Army's lease was terminated in August, 1944, but the brave little slim-gauge pike still rolls freight and passenger trains into the heart of the Yukon.

MOOSE GOOSER
(A.R.R.)

Up through the heartland of "Seward's Icebox" runs a rugged chunk of railroad, connecting the back country of Alaska with the outside world. Operated by the Department of the In-

CHILLY STOP. White Pass & Yukon train in a dramatic setting. Photo shows entrance to tunnel hacked from solid rock on the climb up White Pass. E. A. Hegg photo, courtesy of Joe Williamson.

terior of the United States, the Alaska Railroad is a vital artery serving the Territory with about 470 miles of main line and 58 miles of branch trackage. Dubbed the "Mt. McKinley National Park Route," the trains operated over the road are nicknamed "Moose Goosers" by the natives, and with good cause. The wild moose that inhabit the region cause an operational hazard, especially in winter. When the deep snows blanket the region, the snow plows are hurled into action and cut a narrow highway through the drifts. Intended for the use of trains, the easy going along the cleared right of way proves a great temptation to the strolling moose and they frequently exercise their rights of prior occupation to use the tracks as their personal game trail.

The Alaska Railroad is the outgrowth of two earlier rail lines. The first of these parent roads was chartered on May 3, 1902, as the Alaska Central Railway Company. This ambitious outfit projected about 493 miles of railroad, and

started their construction at the seaport of Seward. By the fall of 1905, the Alaska Central was opened from Seward to Mile 45, and considerable grading had been completed between mile 45 and Mile 105. The road had 350 horses and a number of side dump construction cars, in addition to 4 locomotives, 30 flat cars, 10 box cars and cabooses, and a snow plow. The first

FRIGID SPAN. Engine 152 of the Government Railroad, now the Alaska Railroad, crossed the Tanana River at Nenana on temporary tracks laid on the ice, prior to completion of the bridge at that point. (University of Alaska Museum Photograph)

RAIL MEETS RIVER. Freight train of narrow-gauge White Pass & Yukon delivers machinery and supplies to sternwheelers at Bennett, B.C. Steamboats in foreground are the "CLIFFORD SIFTON" and the "BAILEY." (Courtesy British Columbia Provincial Archives)

engines were small, the original one a saddle-tanker, and several of them reputedly had seen previous service in the steamy tropics, coming second-hand from construction work in Panama's Canal Zone.

While the crews of the Alaska Central were spiking down their steel out of Seward, another rail line was taking shape deep in the interior. This second road was the Tanana Valley Railway, the project of Falcon Joslin. By 1905, the narrow gauge saddletank 1-Spot of the Tanana Valley was chuffing between Chena and Ester Junction, where the road branched down to Fairbanks and then to the mouth of Cleary Creek.

Construction on these two lines soon began to lag, and in 1914, a law was enacted to allow the formation of the Government Railroad, to absorb these two lines and complete the system. However, it was not until 1923 that the line was finished between Seward and Fairbanks. The completion was marked by an excursion and

COPPER HAULER. This trim Mikado type ran on the Copper River & Northwestern, hauling out the famed Kennicott copper ore.

fitting ceremonies, attended by President Warren G. Harding, the first President of the United States to ever visit the Territory of Alaska.

The railroad aided greatly in the development of the rich resources of the interior. At Nenana, on the Tanana River, river steamboats connected for the run down to Tanana and the waters of the Yukon. From Matanuska, a short distance above the Cook Inlet port of Anchorage, a 55-mile branch reached out to Palmer, Moose Creek, and Sutton, to tap the Matanuska coal fields. The numerous gold fields of Cache Creek and the placer district near Fairbanks added to the traffic of the line, and a branch from Healy tapped another coal deposit. From Sutton, short branches connected Eska and Jonesville.

When the clouds of World War II loomed on the horizon, a new line was started to provide another seaport terminal for the road on the Gulf of Alaska. Started in 1941, this new road left the original main line on Turnagain Arm and crossed over to the sheltered terminal at Whittier, located on Portage Bay of Prince William Sound. This branch was completed on November 19, 1942. Uninvited guests at the construction camps were the numerous bears that inhabit the Kenai Peninsula.

Operating conditions are rough in the northlands in the winter, and the hardy crews know the rigors of fighting the drifts of snow hurled upon the line by the Arctic blizzards.

However, the warm suns of springtime turn

ANVIL CREEK. Geared locomotive of the Wild Goose Railroad stands in front of tent housing the "Railroad Saloon," north of Nome, Alaska. E. A. Hegg photo, courtesy of Joe Williamson.

the countryside green and wild flowers bloom in profusion beyond the ends of the ties. A great variety of wild birds raise their broods at trackside, and the bear and moose are curious spectators when the trains rumble along the Land of the Midnight Sun.

FARTHEST REACH

Alaska has been the locale of some colorful railroads and her Seward Peninsula cradled an exceptional one. This was the little Wild Goose Railroad, founded about 1889. In that year, one Charles Lane arrived in Nome and formed the Wild Goose Mining & Trading Company. In connection with this Arctic enterprise, the narrow-gauge Wild Goose Railroad was built, extending about 4 miles out of Nome.

The Wild Goose was unique in several respects. It was the northernmost railroad on the North American continent and also the farthest west, lying 500 miles west of the Hawaiian Islands.

In 1904, the Wild Goose Railroad became the Seward Peninsula Railroad. By September of 1905, the little S.P. had 30 miles of track in operation and by October, 1906, the light rails reached Shelton, on the Kuzitrin River.

When the mines began to play out, hard times fell upon the little pike. Saddletanked Engine No. 4 made the final steam run on the road in 1910, and the rolling stock was left to rust along the beach at Nome.

In 1913 the line was sold to a private operator and in 1921, the Territorial Legislature bought the road and extended it to Bunker Hill, declaring it a public highway. When World War II broke, the Army and Air Force moved into the region and imported two used engines from Colorado to serve their installations. These locomotives were scrapped after the war ended, but a portion of the novel road is still used by a gas rail-bus, which operates over approximately 20 of its original 80 miles of 3-foot trackage.

A close rival for the unique laurels of the Wild Goose Railroad was the Council City & Solomon River Railroad. This standard gauge road was built from the Bering Sea port of Council City, slightly south and east of Nome. It served the mines in the area and extended about 8 miles up the Solomon River to Ophir Creek. Its operations were closed in 1938.

Prince William Sound, on the Gulf of Alas-

ALASKA RAILROAD wood-burning Eng. 151 sported a Rushton or "cabbagehead" smokestack when this photo was taken at Fairbanks in 1929

WHITE FURY. Avalanche of snow carried away Bridge 49-3 and part of a train on Alaska Railroad's "loop district" line between Seward and Anchorage in April, 1921. (University of Alaska Museum Photo)

ka, was the scene of a full-fledged railroad war shortly after the turn of the century. Back in the Chitina country lay a vast deposit of rich copper ore. J. P. Morgan and the brothers Gug-

LAND OF THE MIDNIGHT SUN. This awesome structure is the Hurricane Gulch bridge on the Alaska Railroad, taken shortly after completion. A mixed train of the Government Railroad stands on the high span. (University of Alaska Museum Photo)

genheim formed a company to build a rail line from Valdez into the interior, but abandoned the location. A promoter named H. B. Reynolds then organized the Alaska Home Railway of Valdez and attempted to build a line over the route of the original company, through Keystone Canyon. The powerful syndicate interests sought to block them and a pitched battle took place. One man was killed by rifle fire, and the affair was dragged into court.

The Valdez route was abandoned and the Guggenheims made a second start from Katalla, but their wharf and breakwater was washed away.

Meanwhile, Mike Heney, fresh from his White Pass & Yukon construction, started a railroad out of Cordova. In 1908 the Guggenheim interests contracted with him for completion of this road, which became the Copper River & Northwestern Railroad. The tracks followed the Copper River up to its junction with the Chitina, then swung up the Chitina toward Kennicott and McCarthy. The completion of the road was accomplished in 1911 and the first train brought out a cargo of copper ore in bags that was valued at half a million dollars. The mines produced millions but were finally exhausted and the Copper River & Northwestern Railroad was abandoned in 1938.

Empire Builder

BILLY GOAT
(G.N.)

The history of the Great Northern Railway reaches back to early days in Minnesota, beginning with a charter granted to the Minneapolis & St. Cloud Railway in 1856. This project became allied with the St. Paul, Minneapolis & Manitoba Ry., purchasers of the St. Paul & Pacific Railroad, 1st Division, in the 1870's.

Under authority of legislative action, the pioneer roads gathered up by J. J. Hill filed notice in 1889 of a change of name, and thus was born the Great Northern Railway Company.

The story of the Great Northern is the story of James Jerome Hill. The second child of James and Anne Hill, he was born in Ontario Province, Canada, in 1838. He worked as a grocery clerk for a time, then migrated to the United States to seek his fortune, and was soon employed as a "mud clerk" around the steamboat landing at St. Paul, head of Mississippi River trade.

Hill soon began his spectacular rise, becoming agent for various packetboat companies, and, with Norman Kittson, soon was operating a line of steamboats up the Red River of the North.

Biding his time, he bought up the St. Paul & Pacific R.R. during the Panic of 1873, starting his railroad operations that were to earn him the merited title of "The Empire Builder."

He advanced cash for the construction of the Montana Central Railroad, built between Great Falls, Helena, and Butte. His main line from St. Paul reached steadily westward, driving into Devils Lake, Dakota Territory in 1883. Speeding across the prairies, Hill crews averaged 3¼ miles of track laid per working day, and on one occasion, spiked down slightly over 8 miles of rail in one day. The connection was made with the Montana Central shortly after the St. Paul, Minneapolis & Manitoba crossed the Montana border in 1887.

The true goal of Jim Hill's lines was a saltwater terminus on the Pacific, and the work on this western extension was started at Pacific Junction, just west of Havre, Montana, in August of 1890. Hill sought the easiest possible route for his tracks, and dispatched John F. Stevens to locate a route. Stevens discovered Marias Pass in the heart of the Rockies, and it proved to be the lowest crossing between Mexico and Canada, with a ruling grade of only 1.8 per cent.

To cross the rugged Cascade Mountains, a temporary switchback was built, and the last spike on the new transcontinental was pounded home in the snows of January, 1893, near Scenic, Washington.

REACHING WEST, a string of flat cars deliver rails to "the front" as the Hill road crosses the broad plains of Montana. Locomotive is No. 155 of the St. Paul Minneapolis & Manitoba Railway, and carries an auxiliary water tank coupled behind her tender. Note the blanketed Indians, watching, center foreground. (Courtesy of Historical Society of Montana)

HOME ON WHEELS. These outfit cars were used as living quarters by Jim Hill's railroad crews during construction of the Great Northern across Montana. Initials on the cars stand for St. Paul, Minneapolis & Manitoba, a Hill line subsidiary. Note buffalo skull and deer horns on bunk car at extreme left. (Courtesy of Historical Society of Montana)

"YIM" HILL'S BOYS. These stalwarts are laying track on the main line of the Great Northern Railway in Montana when the "Big G" was pushing its steel west from the Dakota prairies to the salt chuck of Puget Sound. (Courtesy of Historical Society of Montana)

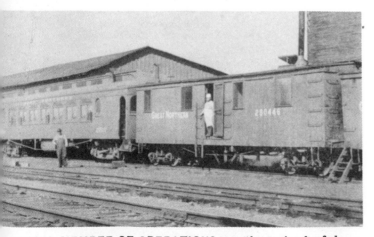

VITAL MEMBER OF OPERATIONS was the cook who fed track gangs and maintenance crews from his kitchen on wheels. This kitchen car was side-tracked on the Great Northern at Odessa, Washington, when the "gut robber" posed for the photographer.

The steep grades of the switchbacks made operation of the 834-mile western extension difficult, and in 1900 the Cascade Tunnel was holed through, the bore being 2.7 miles long. This tunnel cut the grade to 2.2 per cent, and served until a new tunnel, 7.79 miles long, was completed in 1929.

Unlike the other early roads, Hill built his Great Northern without Government aid or land grants, securing financial aid here and abroad. So competently did Hill manage his affairs that when the Panic of 1893 sent most of his competitors into bankruptcy, the Great Northern weathered the storm without failure. Hill was a man of vision, realizing that a railroad must do more than just run trains. He urged immigrants to settle and plant crops, and the road aided in colonization and the introduction of better breeding stock and improved agricultural practices.

The Hill dream began to pay off, elevators springing up along the line, and heavy trains of wheat clattered over the Great Northern tracks. Hill cut the rate on lumber shipments, and soon drags of timber products from the virgin forest of the Northwest were pounding east behind Hill's coal-burners.

Tea and silk trains from Puget Sound sped east, often exceeding passenger train schedules, and these "hot-shots" were the pride of Hill's train and engine crews.

To enlarge the territory served by the Great Northern, many branches were built and short lines added to the fold, either by purchase or by controlling interest in stocks.

The Great Northern purchased the entire capital stock of the Seattle & Montana Railroad and began to operate the line on August 1, 1898. The Seattle & Montana was incorporated in 1890, and built north from Seattle toward Burlington, connecting with the Great Northern's western extension at Everett. The first overland passenger train of the Great Northern left Seattle over this route in June, 1893, passing up the Snohomish and Skykomish valleys to Stevens Pass.

Terminal facilities for the Hill rail and steamship lines were established on the shores of Elliott Bay.

In 1891, the Great Northern secured control of the New Westminster & Southern Ry. and the Fairhaven & Southern, forming a vital link in the shore line system of rails to the Canadian border. Later, the Great Northern acquired the properties of the Seattle & Northern Railway,

SALT WATER TERMINAL. Seattle's railroad yards looked like this shortly after Jim Hill's trains began to operate into the Puget Sound port. (Courtesy of Joe Williamson)

LAST SPIKE in the construction of Great Northern Railway's transcontinental line is hammered home amid winter snows not far from Scenic, Washington, on January 6, 1893. (Courtesy of Great Northern Ry.)

GREET NORTHERN RY. passenger train being "see-sawed" up the Cascade Mts. switchback in western Washington by 3 locomotives in the 1890's. Four levels of track are visible; switchback was replaced by tunnel in 1900. (G. N. Ry.)

and integrated this line into the Anacortes and Rockport lines, in 1902.

East of the Cascades, the "Billy Goat," nick-named for the Rocky Mountain goat depicted on its emblem, had its fingers in a number of other railroad pies. The proprietary Spokane Falls & Northern Railway was opened between Spokane and the International Boundary in 1893, covering 130 miles. In the same year, this line was extended to Troup Junction by the subsidiary Nelson & Fort Shepard Railway, where connections were made into Nelson, B.C., via the Canadian Pacific.

The Columbia & Red Mountain Railway was opened from Northport, Washington, to the International Boundary in 1896, connecting there with the Red Mountain Railway, a subsidiary that built into Rossland, British Columbia.

The Great Northern advanced the cash to build two other lines in the region. One of these was the Washington Great Northern Railway, which opened 27 miles of track from Marcus, Washington, to Laurier, British Columbia, in 1902. The second line was the Vancouver, Victoria & Eastern Railway & Navigation Company, which ran from Laurier to Grand Forks, with lines serving Danville, Copper Junction, Phoenix, and Granby Smelter. An extension of this line dips back down into Washington, terminating at Republic.

The extension of the line from Grand Forks, B.C., to Republic, Washington, was made by two companies. The Kettle River Valley Railway built from Grand Forks to the "Line," while the road from the boundary to Republic was built by the Spokane & British Columbia Railway. Both roads were operated as the "Kettle Valley Lines."

132

SPOKANE FALLS & NORTHERN RAILWAY ran from Spokane to the International Boundary, where it connected with the Nelson & Fort Sheppard Railway to reach Troup Junction; S. F. & N. trains reached Nelson, B.C., where this photo of Engine 3 was taken, by operating over Canadian Pacific trackage from Troup Jct. to Nelson, a distance of about 5 miles. (Courtesy of Fred Jukes)

The Washington Great Northern Ry. and the Vancouver, Victoria & Eastern Ry. & Nav. Co. projected a line from Midway, via Oroville, Keremeos, and Princeton, to Vancouver, B.C., and some work was done, but the line was never completed. The trains of the Great Northern reach Hedley, B.C., (18 miles above Keremeos) by the line from Wenatchee that passes up through Chelan and Omak to Oroville.

The Great Northern owned nearly all the capital stock of the Kootenay Railway & Navigation Company, including the Kaslo & Slocan Railway, Bedlington & Nelson Railway, and the Kootenai Valley Railway, the latter extending from Bonner's Ferry, Idaho, to the International Boundary.

The shaggy-bearded old Empire Builder hated waste and inefficiency in any operation. As a result, the Great Northern had easy grades and curves, with powerful motive power.

Hill and his wife, the former Mary Mehegan, raised a family of six girls and three boys. All of the sons had a whirl at the railroad business, but Louis W. Hill was the only one to make a

SPOKANE FALLS & NORTHERN'S ENGINE 7 was a neat 4-4-0 coal-burner, as shown in this photo at Nelson, B.C., in 1902. The S. F. & N. Ry. and the connecting Nelson & Fort Sheppard Railway were controlled by Hill's Great Northern Railway. Road owned 11 locomotives in 1906. (Courtesy of Fred Jukes)

GREAT NORTHERN'S 155 and 219 at New Whatcom, now Bellingham, in 1897 The 155, pilot bar coupler askew was built by the Brooks works; the 219 was a product of the Rogers factory. (Both photos, courtesy of Fred Jukes)

career of the work. He served the Great Northern for many years, as president and as chairman of the board.

Jim Hill was a versatile man, equally at home in the barn lot of a Swede farmer in Minnesota, the plush sanctum of J. P. Morgan, or the murky interior of a Great Northern roundhouse.

Hill died in 1916, but the Great Northern remains as his permanent monument. When the Great Northern established a crack luxury passenger train on the overland run in 1929, it was christened the "Empire Builder" and the name is perpetuated to this day.

The "Big G" has always had a lot of rough railroading to contend with. The snows of winter hampered the road in the Rockies as well as in the Cascades, and long snowsheds were constructed to prevent the drifts and slides from blocking the road.

A slide in the Cascades set the stage for one of the great runs on the "Big G" in 1899. The Hill road was competing with the Northern Pacific for the Government mail contract and a November slide blocked the east-bound train high in the Cascade Mountains. The mail was packed around the slide and the precious bags were rushed east by a special train.

The Great Northern had received a new batch of fast-stepping 10-wheelers earlier in the year. These engines were built by the Rogers Loco. Works, had 73-inch drivers, and could really turn a wheel. Engineer Jack Croke climbed into the cab of one of these, No. 905, at Leavenworth, Washington, and roared out of town, coupled to a box car loaded with mail and a caboose. The mail slid to a halt in Spokane in four hours flat after leaving Leavenworth, having covered 197 miles. The story of Jack Croke's speedy run was often retold by G.N. crews.

Not all of the 900 class engines were so fortunate, however. One of them, No. 965, ploughed into a mud slide north of Blaine in 1912, and plunged over a bank, killing her fireman and injuring the engineer.

The march of progress has just about written "finis" to the steam locomotive on the Great Northern. Diesels have even driven the big electric "juice jacks" from the electrified zone in the Cascade Mountains, where once "Yim Hill's" engine crews were nearly suffocated by the heat and coal gas in the old tunnel.

The memory of the "Billy Goat" power will linger for some time, however, thanks to the Great Northern's generosity. The city of Wenatchee received a king-sized gift from the old Hill road in 1956. Engine No. 1147, an old slide-valved 2-8-0 built by the Rogers Works in 1902, was presented to the city for permanent exhibition in a park Shiny with new paint, the old freight hauler delights the hearts of small fry and mists the eye of oldsters, who recall the days when Sand Coulee cinders sprinkled the right of way and the "Billy Goat" blasted up to Chumstick or struggled out of Hillyard.

THE WELLINGTON DISASTER

One of the worst disasters in Northwest railroad history took place on the Great Northern Railway on March 1st, 1910.

The preceding months had seen the line plagued by snow storms and blizzards that had piled the snow 30 feet deep on the summit of the Cascades. In the last days of February a warm Chinook swept the mountains and the Inland Empire, causing a number of minor slides and wash-outs. Rail traffic was slowed to a crawl as Great Northern crews battled the

134

THE HAUGHTY AND THE HUMBLE. Great Northern 8-wheeler 224, upper, heads a string of varnish at Bellingham, Wash., in 1905. Lower photo shows G.N. Hinkley-built switch engine No. 30 at the same place in the same year. Note the hinged coupler on pilot of No. 224. (Both photos, courtesy of Fred Jukes)

drifts with rotary snowplows. The Chinook that blew in on the heels of the last blizzard was the villain that set the stage for the Wellington disaster.

On February 25th, 1910, an avalanche near the east portal of the G.N.'s Cascade Tunnel swept away a cook shack, killing two men employed there, but this was only a curtain-raiser for the tragedy that was to come.

Trains 27, the Fast Mail, and No. 25, the Local Passenger, left Spokane for Seattle on February 22nd. By the next day they had arrived at Leavenworth and were delayed until February 25th, while the line through Tumwater Canyon was being opened. On that day the ill-fated trains arrived at the east portal of the old tunnel; two days later, on the night of February 27th, they passed through the tunnel and were halted on the ledge near the west portal, at Wellington station, due to more slide blockades.

Three of the tracks at Wellington were now all occupied. On the track nearest the mountainside stood the private car of Supt. J. H. O'Neill, of the Everett Division, two box cars, three electric motors used in the tunnel, and several locomotives. On the next track stood the local, No. 25, consisting of engine, baggage car, two coaches, two sleepers, and an observation car. On the track nearest the canyon stood the Fast Mail, Train No. 27.

There was food on hand to feed the crews and passengers, but the engines were short of fuel so the trains were not backed into the comparative safety of the tunnel a half mile to the rear. Slides continued to crash and roar down the surrounding mountains, and eight men, including Supt. O'Neill, struck out on foot for Scenic Hot Springs on the western slope to spur efforts to rescue the stalled trains.

On the night of March 1st the hand of Fate struck her cruel blow. A raging gale howled through the canyon, accompanied by sheets of rain and dazzling flashes of lightning. Without warning, a huge avalanche broke loose 1,000 feet above the stalled trains, sweeping down with the speed of a shot. The stranded trains and their pathetic cargo of human lives were swept over the narrow ledge and buried in a jumbled mass of trees, snow, rocks, and twisted railroad equipment in the gorge 200 feet below. The death toll was placed at 101 and the tragedy cost the Great Northern an estimated million and a half dollars.

The gruesome task of digging out the bodies had to be done manually with shovels, picks, and axes. The use of dynamite was declined for fear of further mutilating the victims. The bodies, as they were discovered, were wrapped in tarpaulins and hauled down off the mountain on crude toboggans.

In addition to the passengers, many of the dead were Great Northern laborers, train crews, and postal clerks from the mail train.

The Great Northern officials were shocked by the tragedy and they turned back the swarm of newsmen and photographers who tried to reach the scene. It was not until March 13th that the line was finally re-opened by a small army of railroaders battling away from each side of the lofty Cascades.

GREAT NORTHERN'S ENG. 1106 sported a novel extension on smoke stack in 1902 in attempt to protect crew from heat and smoke in original Cascade Tunnel. The 2.63 mile bore built in 1900 supplanted by 7.79 mile bore in 1929. (G. N. Ry.)

EARLY ROTARY. This rotary snow plow was Southern Pacific's No. 2, the year 1890. Similar plows were in use on the Great Northern at the time of the sad disaster at Wellington. (Courtesy of Southern Pacific)

NORTH BANK ROAD

Ever since Lewis and Clark followed its broad flow down to the Pacific, white men have used the mighty Columbia as a highway.

When Henry Villard was building his Oregon Railway & Navigation line east, he laid his rails on the water level grade up the Columbia's south shore.

The north bank of the river lay dormant, served only by river steamers, until after the turn of the century. Survey parties had passed along the north shore and a number of proposed railroads had been traced along the rocky banks on paper, but the only sound of locomotive whistles were the echoes from the O.R.&N. engines on the Oregon side.

A visitor at Portland's Lewis & Clark Centennial Exposition, held in 1905-06, was James J. Hill. He casually remarked that Oregon was a great state, and that he intended to help in its development. This statement, aired by the press, caused uneasiness in the sanctums of Edward H. Harriman. The Union Pacific-Southern Pacific lines, under Harriman's control, had a virtual monopoly on Oregon's railroads and did not relish the threat of Hill competition.

The bewhiskered old Empire Builder lost no time after his declaration. On August 22, 1905, the Portland & Seattle Railway Company was incorporated to build a railroad from Portland to Spokane, the road to be jointly owned by the Great Northern Railway and the Northern Pacific Railway.

Hill had more at stake than a share of the traffic being handled by the Union Pacific up the Columbia. The Pacific Coast Extension of the Milwaukee Road was authorized in late 1905 and the unoccupied north bank of the Columbia offered a tempting route to the directors of the Chicago, Milwaukee & St. Paul.

On the north bank, Harriman squared off to block Hill cold in his new venture. The major battle was staged at Cape Horn, where a huge barrier of basalt jutted out into the river. Crews of the two rival roads each started a tunnel through this rocky promontory and actual armed warfare developed before the courts decided in favor of the Hill interests. More legal battles raged over the section of the old north shore portage road right of way, still owned by the Harriman interests, but the Portland & Seattle won permission to construct their new road.

Jim Hill's Engines

THE NORTH BANK ROAD, Spokane, Portland & Seattle Ry. operated a fleet of trim steam locomotives such as ten-wheeler No. 150.

STATION SWITCHING. A Great Northern fireman, leaning from cab window, watches for signals while 10-wheeler No. 299 does the chores at Burlington, Washington. (Courtesy of Fred Jukes)

POWER IN ACTION. A big 2-8-8-0 type steamer of the Great Northern gets under way with a tonnage freight train. (Courtesy of H. H. Arey)

SLEEK DUO. No. 150, a 4-6-0- type, and No. 302, a 4-8-0 type, were turned out for the Great Northern by the Brooks Locomotive Works in the 1890's. Note the clean lines and smooth exterior finish, also arched cab windows. (Both photos, courtesy of Fred Jukes)

JIM HILL'S POWER. The Great Northern's No. 1012 (upper) is a good example of the ultimate development of the classic Ten-wheeler. No. 1451, (lower) is a 4-6-2 Pacific type, equipped with a smoke deflector on stack. Both engines sport spoked wheels on leading trucks, and utilize Belpaire fireboxs.

COLUMBIA RIVER & NORTHERN RAILWAY ran from Goldendale to Lyle, Washington, and was connected with Dalles, Portland & Astoria Navigation Co., the famous "Regulator Line" of river steamboats. Engine 1, shown here, was ex-O. R. & N. No. 44, later became Spokane, Portland & Seattle No. 51, and was the first locomotive to enter Goldendale.

DAVID AND GOLIATH. Big 900 class steamer of the Spokane, Portland & Seattle Ry. dwarfs little gear-driven "PONY," first locomotive in the Pacific Northwest. (Photo-Art Commercial Studios photograph)

RAIL CAR. S.P.&S. No. 1103 was a passenger coach driven by a gas engine. (Courtesy of John T. Labbe)

FIRST THROUGH TRAIN over the Astoria & Columbia River Railroad ready to leave Astoria for Portland on May 16th, 1898. Courtesy of Spokane, Portland & Seattle Ry.

With the legal disputes settled, the section between Vancouver and Pasco was opened with appropriate spike ceremonies at Mile Post 50½, near Wind Mountain in the Columbia Gorge. The event took place on March 11, 1908, and the line from Pasco into Spokane was completed in 1909.

Upriver in Klickitat County, a group of Goldendale citizens formed the Columbia Valley & Goldendale Railroad in 1889 and employed R. A. Habersham to run a survey through the Horse Heaven country into Pasco. This company merged with a Pasco group and organized the Pasco, Goldendale & Columbia Valley Railroad. These projects lacked financial backing and collapsed, but the Columbia River & Northern Railroad started a line out of Lyle, Washington, in 1902 and built the 43 miles of track up to Goldendale, completing it in April, 1903. This road was sold to the Northern Pacific in 1905 and transferred to the Portland & Seattle in 1908.

While the Portland & Seattle was grading up the Columbia, another Hill road was stretching

south from Portland up the Willamette Valley. This road was the Oregon Electric Railway and it extended south through Salem and Albany to Eugene, with a short branch to Forest Grove.

The Hill interests in Oregon were consolidated under the operational control of the reorganized Portland & Seattle road, which had emerged as the Spokane, Portland & Seattle Railway.

The oldest line in the new system was the trackage from Portland to Seattle by way of Astoria. This route was composed of three segments; the line from Portland down the Columbia to Goble was originally the Astoria & Coast, and from Goble to Astoria the steel had been laid in 1898 by A. B. Hammond's Astoria & Columbia River Railroad. South from Young's Bay and across the coastal Clatsop Plains to Seaside the new road operated over the 15 miles of track completed in 1890 by the Astoria & South Coast Railway. A short extension beyond Seaside carried the trains to a wye at Holladay, location of the famed Holladay House resort. The Great Northern interests purchased this route from Portland to the seashore in 1907 and passed it into the hands of the Spokane, Portland & Seattle.

The S.P.&S. also operates the old Oregon Trunk line up the Deschutes from Wishram to Bend, and the Oregon Electric trackage, including the old United Railways line to Vernonia and Keasey. Operating over Southern Pacific tracks from Albany to Lebanon, S.P.&S. trains gain access to their Santiam Branch which runs from Lebanon to Sweet Home and Foster, with a short branch to Dollar. Another short branch leaves the Seaside line at Warrenton to serve Flavel and Hammond.

CANYON WAR

High in the Cascade Mountains of Oregon, the Deschutes River springs to life and flows northward through the great inland plateau on its way to the mighty Columbia. Joining forces with the Crooked River, the Deschutes has been busy for centuries, carving a channel through the broken terrain until it now flows through the canyon that bears its name.

The great central Oregon plateau was a rich storehouse of natural resources, and pioneer settlers were soon established there. Grain farms, sheep, cattle and horse ranches dotted the arid region, and virgin forests of huge pine timber clothed the eastern slope of the Cascades and covered the Ochocos.

The great drawback to the settlers was the lack of adequate transportation. The Deschutes was too swift and torturous for navigation, and anything grown or used in the vast region that could not walk to market had to be hauled. Huge freight wagons and trailers, pulled by teams of horses, carted the grain and wool north to the Columbia, returning laden with supplies for the ranchers.

The ranchers petitioned for railroad service, but the pleas fell on deaf ears.

Edward H. Harriman controlled both the Union Pacific and Southern Pacific systems in the early 1900's, and made no move to tap the rich trade of Central Oregon.

One of the prominent cattlemen in the region was William Hanley, commonly called the "Sage of Harney County." Bill Hanley began to stir up Oregon's political pot to build a railroad east of the Cascades, and before long, he was invited to St. Paul, Minnesota, to confer with J. J. Hill, ruler of the Great Northern.

The Hill interests had just completed the North Bank Road down the Columbia, and the old Empire Builder was looking for new terri-

SPOKANE, PORTLAND & SEATTLE'S No. 356 eases coaches down incline at Clarke to meet veteran Snake River and Upper Columbia River steamer, "NORMA." (Courtesy of E. D. Culp)

tory. Harriman smelled a Hill venture in the offing, and he formed the Deschutes Railway Company in 1909. Hill immediately picked up the challenge and formed the Oregon Trunk Railway, and the battle was on.

The forces arrayed themselves and each began grading up the rocky canyon of the Deschutes. Harriman appeared to have the edge on Hill, as the Columbia Southern roughly paralleled the new route, furnishing the Deschutes Railway with a supply line. Hill promptly put the sternwheeler "NORMA" to work, ferrying supplies across the Columbia from Clarke, now Wishram, Washington. He also boated supplies up to The Dalles and shipped them over the Great Southern Railway, recently completed from the port at The Dalles to Dufur.

For his generals in the canyon war, Hill picked some of the best talent on his staff. Chief was John F. Stevens, who had located the original Great Northern passes for the main line. He was ably assisted by Ralph Budd, later famous as a railroad president.

Harriman matched this team with George W. Boschke, builder of Galveston's famed sea wall, and H. A. Brandon, fresh from Harriman relocations.

Hill's contracts were let to Porter Brothers' construction firm, while the Harriman contracts were held by Twohy Brothers. Each force consisted of about 3,000 men, mainly Austrians, Italians, and Swedes, with a scattering of Greek and Slavic laborers and some Americans.

Strange things began to happen along the Deschutes. Boulders rolled down from the high

SLEEK JUICE JOB. Fancy observation car named "CHAMPOEG" decorates the rear end of this Eugene-Portland passenger train on the Oregon Electric Railway. Photo was taken in down-town Salem; second from left is Brakeman George Owen, an O.E. veteran who started with the road in construction days. (Courtesy Mrs. Annie Owen)

SEAPORT TERMINAL. Engine 17 halts with a passenger train at the Astoria station on the old Astoria & Columbia River Railroad. Not far from here, in the winter of 1805-06, Lewis and Clark's party of explorers camped near the shores of their goal, the Pacific Ocean.

PORTLAND BOUND, this is the first train up from Astoria over the Astoria & Columbia River Railroad in May, 1898. Engine being wooded up is one the Hammond road leased from the Oregon & California Railroad, a Baldwin numbered 1361. (Courtesy of Oregon Historical Society)

CLAM DIGGER. Astoria & Columbia River Eng. 4 served lower Columbia River area. Locomotive was acquired second-hand from Corvallis & Eastern Railroad, was a woodburner converted to coal.

NORTH BANK FINALE. Last spike on the Spokane, Portland & Seattle Railway is driven at Sheridan's Point, beside the Columbia, on March 11, 1908. Courtesy of Spokane, Portland & Seattle Ry.

OREGON TRUNK CANTILEVER, designed by Ralph Modjeski, nears completion over Crooked River gorge in 1911. The 340-foot single arch towers 320 feet above the water and was highest single span in America when completed. Courtesy of Spokane, Portland & Seattle Ry.

bluffs into camps, and a case of giant powder with a lighted fuse was discovered in a Deschutes Railway camp. Not long after, the engineers' field headquarters of the Oregon Trunk were burglarized. Grade stakes were pulled up and went bobbing down the trout-filled rapids of the Deschutes.

The hard rock formations made steam shovels nearly useless, and the ones in use, as well as rolling stock of the work trains, were sabotaged by the application of emery dust to the bearings and journal boxes. Near Sherar's Bridge, blasts set off by the Oregon Trunk's crew blew so many fragments of rocks on the gangs of the Deschutes Railway that they were temporarily forced to withdraw.

Many forms of strategy were used by the rival lines. Boschke, Harriman's leader, received a mysterious telegram, supposedly sent from Galveston, Texas. It stated, "Come at once. The sea wall has broken." The veteran engineer scoffed and shredded the message, stating that he had built that structure to last.

Armed "troops" from both camps faced each other at a crucial spot where the Canyon narrowed so close there was scarcely room for one railroad, let alone two.

When it reached the point where a pitched battle seemed imminent, R. S. Lovett, president of the Harriman lines, held a personal conference with James J. Hill. As a result, a truce was called and an amicable settlement conclud-

THE BATTLEFIELD. A view of the track on the Deschutes Railroad, showing where the Harriman forces hacked a right of way along a solid rock bluff in their race with Hill's Oregon Trunk up the Deschutes Canyon.

BIG DIPPER. Steam shovel loads gravel for ballast onto flat cars coupled to Astoria & Columbia River R.R. No. 3 during construction near Goble, Oregon. (Angelus Studio Photograph)

HORSESHOE CURVE. Hill and Harriman crews raced to lay their steel along the Deschutes, shown here near Sinamox station. Courtesy of Spokane, Portland & Seattle Ry.

ed in 1910. The lines combined forces and the Deschutes Railway was to be granted permanent traffic lights into Bend over the steel of the Oregon Trunk.

It was a great day for Central Oregon when the final spike was pounded home at Bend on October 5, 1911. Jim Hill and his son, Louis, were among the honored guests of the day, and when the final spike had been driven and then pulled up, Jim Hill slipped it into the pocket of big Bill Hanley, pioneer ranchman who had worked so long to secure a steel highway for his beloved rangelands.

In later years, the Great Northern built south from Bend to Chemult, where the G.N. trains passed onto Southern Pacific tracks for the run into Klamath Falls. From the latter point Great Northern rails were laid through the historic Modoc country to Bieber, California, where traffic is turned over to the connecting Western Pacific for shipment into San Francisco.

During the struggle between the titans, Hill interests acquired the Medford & Crater Lake Railroad in 1909. This short line built out from Medford to Butte Falls, starting in 1905, and Hill intended to use it as a link between his Oregon Trunk and a proposed extension to the coast at Crescent City, California. From the latter point, it would have been possible for him to build down the Redwood Coast to enter San Francisco, but the dream collapsed and the Medford line is operated as a logging railroad at present.

The California extension from Bend was completed in 1931, long after the dust of the Canyon War had settled. Today, trains of fat white-faced Herefords, wooly sheep, golden grain, and pungent pine lumber rumble down the canyon of the Deschutes, scene of the bitter strife a short 50 years ago.

SHAGGY OLD EMPIRE BUILDER. James J. Hill surveys a part of his railroad domain in the Northwest from the back seat of an early auto. Photo was taken at depot in Vancouver, Wash., about the time the Spokane, Portland & Seattle Ry. was completed. (Courtesy of Spokane, Portland & Seattle Ry.)

Steel To The Seashore

BELOVED CLAMSHELL

The southwest tip of Washington Territory was the scene of considerable activity in the spring of 1888. The screeching of the gulls circling the wharf at Ilwaco, tucked back behind Sand Island on Baker Bay, was disturbed by the tooting of a locomotive. Spike mauls echoed as steel banged steel, and construction was under way on one of the most picturesque of all Northwest short lines.

Lewis A. Loomis, a New York farm boy, had arrived at Oysterville, Washington Territory, in 1872. In 1874 Loomis had been instrumental in forming the Ilwaco Wharf Co. and building a wharf at Ilwaco. This venture boomed and in 1875 a new corporation was formed, doing business as the Ilwaco Steam Navigation Company. Loomis soon was awarded the contract for carrying the mails between Astoria and Olympia, W.T., and in 1881 formed the Shoalwater Bay Transportation Company, acquiring the steamboats "Gen. Miles" and "Gen. Garfield."

Perhaps his experiences with railroads during the Civil War influenced Loomis in his decision to provide a rail line from Ilwaco north up the Long Beach peninsula; at any rate the Il-waco Steam Navigation Co. raised some money by increasing its stock and Major A. F. Searles was hired to run a preliminary survey. Searles made the survey and recommended that the road be made a narrow-gauge to keep down construction costs.

Loomis had succeeded in gaining the assistance of Jacob Kamm to aid in the venture and the choice was a wise one. Together they engaged Harvey Pike to lay out a final survey and this was completed in 1887.

By March of 1888 the town of Ilwaco boasted an engine house, water tank, shops, depot, and turntable, along with a stretch of track that ran down the center of the main street from the wharf. Shortly after, the first rolling stock arrived. Engine No. 1 was a Baldwin 2-6-0 type, built in 1879 as the No. 15 of the Utah Northern Railroad. The Utah Northern had renumbered her No. 19 before selling her to the Ilwaco Steam Nav. Co. for $2,500. She was to serve the road faithfully until scrapped in 1911.

The new engine helped speed construction and the raw grade north through the sand dunes unearthed quantities of clam shells, which in turn gave rise to the road's nickname, the "Clamshell." By July of 1888 the sixty-pound

BELCHING BLACK SMOKE, an Ilwaco Ry. & Nav. Co. engine laboriously drags a long string of passenger coaches away from the dock at Megler, bound for Ilwaco and Nahcotta. A second section is still loading at the right of the depot and warehouse; steamer that has brought loads of vacationers down from Portland is hidden by the clouds of smoke. (Courtesy of Union Pacific R.R.)

ILWACO RAILWAY & NAVIGATION CO. crews had Engine No. 4 all slicked up when this photo was taken on the long wharf at Ilwaco, Washington. Slim-gauge diamond-stacker was burning wood at this time. She had come to the "Clamshell" from Portland & Willamette Valley Ry., who in turn had acquired her from the Utah & Northern, where she had been number 19, later U.P. 23. Note logs loaded on standard flat cars. (Photo by Ford, Ilwaco, Wn.)

steel had reached Long Beach and a grand excursion held to celebrate the occasion.

On August 6, 1888, the newly-former Ilwaco Railroad & Navigation Co. took over the holdings of the Ilwaco Steam Navigation Co. and the track crept north through the winter months. In May of 1889 the road reached the northern terminal at Nahcotta on Willapa Bay, thirteen and one-half miles north of Ilwaco. Conductor Robinson and Engineer George Jennings manned the first regular train. Both freight and passenger business was good, the

ILWACO RAILWAY & NAVIGATION CO. Engine No. 2 stands ready to leave Nahcotta terminal with a passenger train. Narrow-gauge locomotive was built new for the road by H. K. Porter Loco. Works in 1890, was scrapped in 1908. Launch at left is the "NASELLE" and hauled mail and passengers to connect with I. R. & N. trains.

oyster industry shipping great cargoes of the succulent bivalves from Willapa to Ilwaco.

With the increasing loads another locomotive was needed and Vice-Pres. Jacob Kamm personally watched a portion of the construction of Eng. No. 2 at the Porter, Bell & Co. Loco. Works in Pittsburgh, Pennsylvania, in April of 1890. New coaches were soon added to the original second-hand equipment.

In May of 1897 an accident took place at the Ilwaco terminal when a section of the dock gave way, plunging the engine, a box car, and the coach into six feet or so of salty tidewater. No one was seriously injured and little damage done to anything except the reputation of an I.R.&N. official; trapped in the coach with seven passengers, he is reputed to have cried out, "Save me first! I am a company officer!"

The Gay Nineties saw a great increase in the swarms of vacationists who flocked to the beaches up the peninsula and in 1892 Jacob Kamm launched the elegant sidewheel steamer, "Ocean Wave," to convey these throngs from Portland directly to the Ilwaco dock. Controversy over the operation of the steamer brought about a split between Loomis and Kamm; the Oregon Railroad & Navigation Co. quietly bought up Kamm's stock and Loomis was pressured into selling his interests to them in 1900.

Business continued good and for a time the

road enjoyed a lucrative log traffic, hauling them from Willapa Bay to a log dump on Ilwaco's wharf, but the perfection of sea-going log rafts soon put an end to this traffic. An obstacle in the road's operation was the shifting sandbars that blocked the connecting steamers entering Baker Bay; boat schedules and the railroad timetable had to be adjusted in order to take advantage of flood tides to enable the vessels to reach the dock.

In 1906 the O.R.&N. formed a subsidiary company, the Columbia Valley Railroad, to construct a line from Cook's Station, east of Point Ellice, to a junction with the narrow-gauge near Ilwaco.

In 1907 a new corporation, the Ilwaco Railroad, was formed and later in the year the old Ilwaco Railway & Navigation Co. was added to the properties of the new Ilwaco Railroad. The new extension from Ilwaco Junction east to Megler, slightly over 13 miles, was finally completed in June, 1908. The boggy terrain and the hard-rock tunnel under Fort Columbia had both been difficult problems confronting the construction gangs.

New locomotives had arrived to aid in the task of building the extension up-river to Megler and to pull the additional loads of passengers that flocked to the line after a deep-water dock had been provided. A good dock and depot was

BATTERED AND NEGLECTED, the old No. 1 of the 3-foot gauge Portland & Willamette Valley presents a sorry appearance as she rusts in idleness after Southern Pacific standard-gauged the line. Engine was built in 1880, and was sold in 1906 (after above photo was made) to the Ilwaco Ry. & Nav. Co. where she was numbered 4 and later became second No. 2. I. R. & N. paid $500 for her and she served the Long Beach Peninsula until 1931, when she was scrapped and her boiler sold for use in an Astoria laundry. (Courtesy of D. L. Joslyn)

established at Megler, along with a trainshed and a steel turntable, and depots were built at Chinook and other places. The Nahcotta roundhouse was enlarged and 90-pound steel rails replaced the light 60-pound rail on the original line, a concession to the heavy new Eng. 6, a Baldwin 10-wheeler and the heaviest locomotive on the road.

In 1911 the holdings of the O.R.&N. and other

CLAMSHELL'S PASSENGER TRAIN, standing at narrow-gauge depot at Ilwaco, Wn. Eng. 5 and coach bear initials of Oregon-Washington R.R. & Nav. Co., a subsidiary of Ilwaco Ry. & Nav. Company's owner, Union Pacific. (Angelus Studio photo)

BEANPOLE TRESTLE. Piledriver and bridge carpenters pause during construction of P. R. & N.'s Big Baldwin Creek structure. When completed, this was reputed to be the highest timber trestle in the world.

Union Pacific subsidiaries in the Northwest were merged into a new concern called the Oregon-Washington Railroad & Navigation Co., and the "Clamshell" became the Ilwaco Division of the O-W RR & N. In later years the equipment was re-lettered Union Pacific.

The road owned eight locomotives during its lifetime. No. 1 was scrapped in 1911. No. 2, the Porter Mogul built new for the road in 1890, was scrapped in 1908. No. 3, the oldest engine on the line, was another Porter 2-6-0 that had originally been on the Walla Walla & Columbia River Railroad. After passing to several other companies she was purchased by the I.R.&N. in 1900 for $900; five months later the Ilwaco road sold her to A. J. McCabe for $600.

Engine No. 4 was a Baldwin Mogul purchased by the I.R.&N. from the Southern Pacific's defunct Portland & Willamette Valley Railroad in 1906 at a cost of $500. When the Ilwaco road's power was renumbered by the Union Pacific management, she became Ilwaco Ry. & Nav. Co. No. 2; the ancient steamer was

scrapped in 1931 but even then her years of usefulness were not at an end, for her boiler was put into service in a laundry in Astoria.

Ilwaco's second Eng. No. 3 was a Baldwin eight-wheeler and was acquired from the South Pacific Coast Railroad in California; when the power was renumbered, she became the No. 1. No. 5, another eight-wheeler, and No. 6, the ten-wheeler, also were Baldwin products acquired from the South Pacific Coast. In the Ilwaco renumbering the 5 became No. 3 and the 6 became No. 4. These engines were used until the end of operations.

The invasion of the auto and the decline of the oyster trade brought the pinch of hard times to the road. When the crash of 1929 hit, the Union Pacific pared operations and permission was finally granted to abandon the "Clamshell." The last run of the scheduled mixed train was

PRIMITIVE PILEDRIVER had no power. Hammer was raised by line attached to locomotive, which backed up (after each blow was tripped) to hoist hammer.

made south from Nahcotta on September 9, 1930, with Engineer Clem Morris at the throttle of old No. 2.

Engines 1, 3, and 4 were sold for scrap to a Portland junk dealer and were cut up. No. 2 stayed on the line, her bell tolling the death knell as she helped the scrappers rip up the slim-gauge track. Local residents purchased all 12 passenger cars for use as summer cottages, lunch stands, etc.

The Washington State Highway Department obtained most of the old right-of-way and today autos roar over the grade where once the diminutive locomotives huffed and puffed. Even the tunnel under Fort Columbia was widened to become a part of the highway system.

The lonely gulls wheel and cry over Ilwaco and the noise of the train whistle no longer disturbs their clamourings. The sea breeze sweeps the tang of salt air over the peninsula as it has since Creation, but the pungent aroma of steam and hot valve oil is missing. Look in vain for the narrow ribbon of steel, the pillar of smoke, and the flashing of side-rods . . . the "Clamshell" is no more.

RAT HOLE. Camera looks out toward the Pacific from the interior of P. R. & N.'s Tunnel No. 2, west of Cochran. Trains ran through a trench formed by walls of timber and logging operations were carried on almost within reach of coach windows. Falling trees often blocked trains and crews kept a sharp lookout when running over the crooked line, noted for its many blind curves.

TALL TIMBER AND ROCKY CUTS line the new steel of the Pacific Railway & Navigation Company. Road had not yet been ballasted when this photo was taken during construction through the Coast Range.

PUNK, ROTTEN, AND NASTY

(The Pacific Railway & Navigation Co.)

The picturesque 91-mile Tillamook Branch of the Southern Pacific Company started its existence as the Pacific Railway & Navigation Co., better known to the inhabitants of the rugged section of western Oregon pierced by the line as the "Punk, Rotten & Nasty."

The Coast Range mountains form a tight circle around the town of Astoria, down at the mouth of the Columbia River, and early-day Astorians dreamed of a railroad to the interior. Being civic-minded, they did something about the matter and formed the Astoria & South Coast Railway in 1888. The Astoria & South Coast drove its first spike at Skipanon on May 11th, 1889, and had built 10 miles of road by June when William Ried was chosen as President. A line passing through the Nehalem Valley was selected and grading started at Astoria on the western end and at Hillsboro, located on the Southern Pacific, on the eastern end.

Squabbles between President Ried and vari-

HIGHWAY 101 was a plank road when the Portland-Tillamook "varnish" unloaded crowds of vacationists at Rockaway to stroll beside blue Pacific, visible beyond engine. Improved highways and modern automobiles killed the branch line passenger traffic.

ous Astoria factions brought the work to a halt, but Ried secured English capital and organized the Portland, Nehalem & Astoria Ry. in the fall of 1890.

By January of 1891 Ried had graded seven and one-half miles up the Lewis & Clark River on the west end and eight miles west of Hillsboro. Shortly after, the English capital ran out and the road came to a halt.

William Ried rallied his battered finances and in 1907 formed the Portland, Oregon & Seacoast Ry. to build through the Nehalem Valley but the panic broke him and he died shortly after the collapse of this last effort.

Tillamook was still isolated by bad roads and the vagaries of coastal steamers when Elmer E. Lytle appeared in 1905. Lytle had been a station agent for the Oregon Ry. & Nav. Co. at Waitsburg, Washington, in 1889. In 1897 he became interested in the building of the short line Columbia Southern Railway from Biggs to Shaniko, Oregon. He was President of the C.S.Ry. in 1900 and in 1903 the line was sold to E. H. Harriman of the Union Pacific.

Lytle looked for new fields to conquer and

on October 1, 1905, incorporated the Pacific Railway & Navigation Co., probably with E. H. Harriman's blessing, if not with something more potent, such as cold, hard cash.

E. E. Lytle set up camp at Hillsboro, assisted by C. E. Lytle, and Daniel M. McLauchlan was appointed superintendent. The office was an old passenger coach set down on blocks. A second-hand 4-4-0 type engine arrived, purchased from the Northern Pacific, and was operated by Engineer Charles Follette and Fireman Harry McLauchlan, son of the superintendent. The grade was driven west from Hillsboro, and a short time later the road started construction east from Tillamook. A second 4-4-0 locomotive was purchased from the Southern Pacific and became the PR&N No. 2. No. 2, along with a number of cars, was barged around from Portland to Tillamook Bay and given to Engr. Ed Wilkinson and Fireman Al Wagner. The first section of the line west of Hillsboro was opened for service in 1906, but the Panic of 1907 brought a halt to construction for a time. Work was soon resumed and the steel ribbons of track crept into the rugged terrain of the Coast Range. The track from Tillamook skirted the marshy edges of Tillamook Bay to Barview, then along the shores of the Pacific Ocean to Jetty. Here they turned inland along the south bank of Nehalem Bay and followed up the Nehalem River.

A third locomotive was added to the roster of motive power in 1910 when the road purchased Mogul-type No. 1605 from the Southern Pacific. Out-shopped by the Baldwin Works in 1883, No. 3 was a standard gauge woodburner and there was a plentiful supply of fuel at hand to feed the hungry fireboxes. The line was extending into virgin forests, entirely cloaked with majestic firs of enormous size.

Portable sawmills were moved along the track, cutting the necessary bridge and tunnel timbers from the forest giants that were felled to clear the right-of-way.

The summit of the Coast Range was topped at Cochran, 1,835 feet above sea level. On the western slope of the mountains the two ends of track met near the Twin Bridges and the first train from Portland arrived in Tillamook on October 9, 1911. By November 1st of that year regularly-scheduled trains were operating.

The road had cost about $5,000,000 to build, and it was 91 miles long. The track bored through 13 tunnels, the longest of these being 1,437 feet. The maximum grade was slightly over 3% with some 15-degree maximum curves. There were a great many bridges along the line, the highest one measuring 167 feet, and 35 of them were over 100 feet in length. Among these bridges was one reputed to be the highest single pile span in the world.

The Southern Pacific Co. took over the P.R.&N. in 1915 and is still operating it as the Tillamook Branch of their Portland Division. It proved a rich source of both revenue and headaches. Excursion trains from Portland to the Tillamook County beaches operated every summer until the automobiles and good roads killed the business. Long trains of coaches, jammed to the vestibules with vacationists, struggled up the steep grades with four locomotives blasting their smoke plumes skyward. One unusual feature of operating procedure was that used on a train called the "Rector Logger." This train hauled long drags of logs from the camp at Rector down to the sawmill at the Brighton station on Nehalem Bay. The schedule on which this train departed from Rector with the loads varied in accordance with the tide tables, as it was planned to have the train arrive at the

FOUR LOCOMOTIVES stand panting on head end of passenger train at Cochran, returning summer vacationists from Tillamook County beaches. Virgin forest still towers over track as engineers check their equipment after the long, hard climb up to the summit of the Coast Range. Indicators on leading locomotive identify train as the second section of S.P.'s regular passenger train No. 142.

OLD ONE-SPOT used in building Pacific Railway & Navigation Co. formerly wheeled trains for the Northern Pacific before straying into Western Oregon timberlands.

SEA GULL ROOST is trestle carrying P. R. & N. tracks across tidewater of Tillamook Bay at Bay City. Two spurs on trestlework leading away to left served a sawmill and a fish dock. Main line trestle in foreground was later replaced by a rock and earth fill. (Gregg photo)

153

Timber Profile

Seven views on the Tillamook line of the Southern Pacific in the days when steam ruled the rails.

(No. 1) 2001 on the wye at Buxton, working in helper service.

(No. 2) 2134, waiting to help the second section of Train 150.

(No. 3) 2141, running extra at Timber.

(No. 4) 2500, with "bay window" cab, takes water at Timber tank.

(No. 5) 2141 and 2197, 4-6-0 types, doublehead a passenger train.

(No. 6) 2957, a 4-8-0, gets a helping hand with her freight train from two Consolidation types, Engine 2839 on the point, as she tops the summit of the Coast Range at Cochran.

(No. 7) 2833, a 2-8-0 type, lies amid the wreckage of Little Baldwin trestle after its collapse in 1935. Five railroaders lost their lives in this tragedy.

THE HARD WAY. Gang of men at right are clearing out a cut by hand, shoveling rock and earth onto a flat car to be hauled away.

PACIFIC FURY. Ocean batters P. R. & N. tracks at Barview during winter storm, about 1916. Work train is dumping boulders in effort to save track. Large building in rear is U. S. Coast Guard station.

PILLARS OF SMOKE and steam blast skyward as two Southern Pacific engines "buck" shallow snowdrifts near Cochran on Tillamook Branch about 1916.

LOG CABIN depot serving the village of Timber was a unique but appropriate structure; fireplace that heated the waiting room was built with river-worn rocks. Locomotive at left has just come down from bucking snow over the summit of the Coast Range.

FIRST TRAIN over western end of P. R. & N. in Tillamook County carried excursionists in coach, caboose, and flatcars equipped with temporary benches for sightseers on trip to view the new railroad.

ENGINE 2187 lies in the ditch near Juno after being derailed while backing up. Site of derailment is not far from Tillamook and mishap occurred shortly after S. P. acquired the road from Pacific Ry. & Nav. Co. in 1915. Crew escaped injury by "joining the birds," railroad slang for jumping off. Engine was a product of the Central Pacific Shops, Sacramento, and was built in 1888.

COAST LINE WASHOUT. A plugged culvert and a flooding creek undermined this fill on the P. R. & N., causing engine and a boxcar loaded with Japanese laborers to come to an abrupt but bloodless halt. Accident took place near Jetty station, named for the timber jetty jutting out into ocean at mouth of Nehalem Bay, visible at right in above photo.

MOUNTAIN RAILROADING in the Pacific Northwest called for much engineering ingenuity. Track shown here leaving tunnel crosses high combination trestle and truss bridge in the foreground on a sharp curve and steep grade, a portion of the Wolf Creek "loop" on the Pacific Railway & Navigation Co. Engine crews coming down-grade through tunnel fervently hoped that the fires which frequently raged through the timber had not destroyed this structure; the drop to the brawling waters of Wolf Creek was a long one!

Brighton log dump when the tidewater was high enough to permit the logs to float from the dumping grounds into the log booms.

On the headache side of the ledger was the problem of keeping the road operating. Slides and falling rocks frequently blocked the tracks, especially in the stormy winter months. The gales that came sweeping in from the Pacific toppled giant trees across the line and both passenger and freight trains carried an assortment of axes, saws, and cable to clear these obstructions. In addition, the forest fires that periodically raged through the prime stands of fir, hemlock, spruce, and cedar often threatened the line. In September of 1931 fire roared over forty miles of northwestern Tillamook County. Fires in 1932 and again in 1933 ravaged the region. These fires wiped out the logging camps at Cochran, Ripple, Mayo, and Enright. The Enright depot was burned, three tunnels damaged, and several trestles consumed by the angry red flames that charred over 380 square miles of highly valuable timber lands.

One Consolidation type (2-8-0) engine could only haul 10 loaded cars from Enright to Cochran, making the use of helper locomotives mandatory. These helper engines were based at the mountain village of Timber, a little hamlet perched astride the tracks on a steep hillside. The maximum train permitted over the road was limited to 60 cars and it was a spectacular sight to witness one of these freights battling up the westward slope toward Cochran. Five or six locomotives, two on the head end and the others coupled in toward the rear, all blasted along with widened throttles and reverse levers dropped "down in the corner." Pillars of smoke belched skyward from this collection of power as the train snailed up the crooked track, rarely travelling over 15 miles per hour. The thunder of the engine exhausts put the deer and elk to flight and the chant of the hammering driving wheels announced its coming long before the laboring engines hove into view.

Passenger service was pulled off during the depression, although the daily freight trains carried a coach for the convenience of loggers, hunters, and anglers until recent times. Steam has been banished from the road and a few Diesels now do the work that was the chore of the numerous helper and road locomotives. Efficiency rules the line's operation but the glory and the grand manner of the days of steam are a fragrant memory in the minds of those who saw the P.R.&N. when it was a railroad man's railroad.

Northwest Corner

OLYMPIC FIASCO

The citizens of Port Townsend were highly elated in the early 1870's when it was thought their town might be chosen as the Pacific terminus of the coming Northern Pacific, but the project ended with the failure of Jay Cooke & Co. in 1873.

Discouraged but not beaten, the Port Townsendites got together in 1887 and formed the Port Townsend & Southern Railroad. The company acquired a right of way along the Hood Canal to Olympia, and called for bids on six miles of track on March 23, 1889. Not long after, actual work was started and the first ground was broken on the farm of Judge Briggs, about two miles west of Port Townsend. The prospect of a railroad caused a great boom in Port Townsend and property prices soared. However, the work lagged for lack of funds and it was not until 1890 that much actual construction was accomplished.

The Oregon Improvement Company became interested in the project and on March 12, 1890, a meeting was held in Learned's Opera House and a contract was signed, giving the Oregon Improvement Co. control of the road. The citizens of Port Townsend pledged a bonus of

$100,000 and the new management agreed to have 25 miles of track in operation by September 1st, 1890.

H. W. McNeill was appointed vice president and resident manager and on April 1st a contract was awarded to Hale & Smith for the first 20 miles of track out of Port Townsend. Later in April, McNeill purchased the narrow gauge line that had been built for 10 miles between Olympia and Tenino under the charter of the Olympia & Chehalis Valley Railroad. The Port Townsend Southern paid $192,000 for this section of road, converted it to standard gauge, and extended it four miles from Olympia to deep water on Puget Sound.

By May of 1890, there were 1,500 men at work along the Port Townsend road and a depot and roundhouse erected on a filled swamp west of the town. By August, the trains were running between Port Townsend and Lake Hooker, but the work came to a halt in November of 1890, caused by the failure of the banking house of Baring Brothers of London and the collapse of the Oregon Improvement Company.

Joseph Simon was appointed as receiver for the road and 500 men were back at work in March of 1891. On the 9th of June, Hale &

SATSOP RAILROAD pioneered rail transportation into Shelton, Washington. Eng. 1 is odd 0-4-2 saddle-tank, with Engr. Crow in cab and Supt. Arthur Needham standing on pilot beam. (Courtesy Simpson Logging Co.)

ALL ABOARD! Columbia & Puget Sound Railroad No. 1, the "A. A. DENNY," heads off into the tall timber with an excursion train. Car behind engine is a combination coach and caboose; note the temporary coaches toward rear made by erecting sides and roofs on ordinary flat cars. No. 1 was built by William Mason in 1870, weighed 75,000 pounds, and had 14 x 16 inch cylinders.

Smith finished the 7 miles from Lake Hooker to Quilcene and the 26-mile pike was completed, although far short of its goal. The Pacific Coast Company acquired the properties in 1897 and control passed to the Northern Pacific in 1902. The N.P. operated the Port Townsend Southern as a subsidiary for a number of years.

Close neighbor of the Port Townsend & Southern was the Port Angeles Western, a standard gauge road from the head of Port Discovery Bay to Port Angeles. The road was constructed largely through the efforts of C. J. Erickson, and a 20-mile section west of Port Angeles connected with Mike Earles' logging

SEATTLE WHARF and docks form backdrop for "A. A. DENNY," Eng. No. 1 of Columbia & Puget Sound Railroad, serving King County coal mines. Locomotive is an unusual type, boiler and tender both located on a single frame. Road was originally the Seattle & Walla Walla Railroad.

railroad. This western segment was built first, to convey Earles' logs to a saw mill in Port Angeles. The connection from Port Angeles to the Port Townsend & Southern was completed in 1915.

During the first World War, the Spruce Production Division built a number of railroads in the Northwest, including the 36-mile Clallam County Railroad from Disque Junction, west of Port Angeles, into the timber. Lyon, Hill & Company bought the spruce road in 1923 and it was resold to the Sol Duc Investment Company in 1929. It became a part of the Port Angeles Western, which road had passed to the control of the Milwaukee Road.

HANDS ACROSS THE BORDER

The Bellingham Bay & British Columbia Railroad was formed in 1883 to build from Whatcom (now Bellingham) to the Canadian Boundary and a connection with the lines of the Canadian Pacific Railway. The leader of this project was Pierre B. Cornwall, head of the Bellingham Bay Coal Company, and the road was backed by D. Ogden Mills.

Ground was broken on April 7, 1884, but only a slight amount of progress was made. In October, 1888, the first two locomotives were delivered, along with thirty flat cars and a quantity of rails; these engines were named the "BLACK DIAMOND" and the "D. O. MILLS." Under the direction of L. M. Stangroom, the

COLUMBIA & PUGET SOUND RAILROAD hauled passengers as well as vast amounts of coal. Here No. 12 heads a consist of three coaches, flying the white flags of an extra train. (Courtesy of Fred Jukes)

road was completed to Sumas in March, 1891.

The celebration held in New Whatcom to welcome the first Canadian Pacific train touched off an international incident that resounded in embassies and the Court of St. James.

Elaborate preparations had been made to welcome the train bearing Canadian officials and dignitaries on June 22, 1891. A huge arch, bearing both British and American flags, was erected at Railroad Avenue and Holly Street, and two bands were on tap, along with uniformed fraternal and patriotic groups. As a final touch, it had been arranged to have the fire companies of Whatcom and Sehome play an arch of water over the tracks as the train arrived. All was in readiness, and when the whistle of the special sounded in the distance, both bands burst into full volume and the brave fire laddies manned their respective hoses to form the liquid arch.

However, and whether by accident or intent is still a mystery, somebody's fire hose squirted the hosemen on the opposite side of the track. Instantly, a full-fledged water fight was in progress. The special came chuffing into range and a powerful stream of water struck it from either side, breaking out coach windows and thoroughly dousing the occupants. After the deluge of water came a flood of apologies, and the visiting dignitaries were dried out and rushed to Purdy's Opera House for a sumptuous banquet.

When the celebration was at its height, someone in the crowd conceived the idea that the British flag on the big arch was a few inches higher than its American companion. In a burst of patriotic fervor, several youths scrambled up to correct this situation. In the excitement that followed, the Union Jack was torn loose and came fluttering to the ground where it was trampled underfoot. The Canadians were greatly incensed and rolled away home muttering in their whiskers.

The British lion's tail had been twisted and the diplomats of both countries became involved before the results of the unhappy incident were smoothed over.

Under Supt. J. J. Donovan, the B.B.&B.C. started work on an extension up the Nooksack River to Spokane in 1900-01, but this line ended at Glacier. A branch to Lynden was built in 1903, and the Milwaukee Road acquired the entire road in 1911-12.

ENGINE No. 2 of the Bellingham Bay & British Columbia Railroad, an 0-6-0 saddle tank, in front of the road's shops. She bore the name "BLACK DIAMOND." (Courtesy of Fred Jukes)

RARE PHOTO. This fine view of Schenectady-built Engine No. 2 of the Fairhaven & Southern is from the excellent collection of Fred Jukes, pioneer railroad photographer. The engine is shown as she was delivered to the road, surrounded by a group of admirers. (Courtesy of Fred Jukes)

NORTH TO THE LINE

Bellingham Bay, up in Washington's northwest corner, was the scene of considerable feverish railroad activity in the 1880's. In August of 1883, the Bellingham Bay Railroad & Navigation was organized by the Honorable Eugene Canfield, United States Senator from Illinois.

The avowed purpose of Canfield's railroad project was to construct a road from Fairhaven to Sumas, rivalling the new Bellingham Bay & British Columbia Railroad.

After considerable surveying, Canfield dropped that idea and headed his transitmen in the direction of Blaine and New Westminster. The Canadian Pacific Railway had completed an extension to New Westminster in 1886, and Canfield sought to connect with them. In 1888, Canfield formed the New Westminster & Southern. After financial problems arose, the Canadian interests purchased Canfield's share of the New Westminster & Southern and in July, 1889, Canfield sold the paper-work Bellingham Bay Railroad & Navigation Company to Nelson Bennett.

Bennett had been awarded the contract for completion of the New Westminster & Southern, and, dropping the old Canfield vehicle, he proceeded to organize the Fairhaven & Southern Railway.

Work was pushed on this new line under Bennett's chief engineer, J. J. Donovan, and by 1890 the steel was laid between Bellingham Bay and Sedro-Woolley. In March of 1890, word

seeped around that both the Fairhaven & Southern Railway and the New Westminster & Southern Railway had passed into the hands of the energetic James Jerome Hill. Such proved to be the case, but the roads were permitted to retain their separate identities. Work on the northern end of the Fairhaven & Southern was pushed and the road reached Squalicum Creek in August of 1890.

By October, the first engine was hooting into Ferndale. North of Enterprise, the engineers encountered unstable going. One section of grade became known as "The Devil's Bread Pan," due to the constant upheaval of the roadbed. In spite of difficulties there and at the Nikomekl River crossing, the Fairhaven & Southern reached the International Boundary on December 1st, 1890.

South from Bellingham, the Fairhaven & Southern drove into Burlington in 1891 and connected its rails with those of the Seattle & Montana Railroad, a Hill subsidiary. The ex-steamboat clerk now had completed the projects that would form the nucleus for his Great Northern's Shore Route.

In those days of simple amusements it was considered highly fashionable to make railroad excursions and the Good Templars of Fairhaven arranged such a trip to Blaine. Engine 199, pulling the excursion train, struck some scaffolding on the Nooksack River bridge and her graceful smokestack went into the river with a splash. The resourceful crew procured an empty keg,

CAP-STACKED TEN-WHEELER bore the No. 1 designation on the Puget Sound & Baker River Railroad. Engine has old style slide valves operated by Stephenson valve gear; center dome atop boiler was for steam, domes at front and rear contained sand to give the engine traction when rails were slippery.

TRIM PAINT JOB sets off this builder's photo of the Prairie type No. 102 of the Wenatchee Valley & Northern Railway, a Washington short line.

THE "SKOOKUM" was an odd type 2-4-4-2 compound used on Washington's Columbia River Belt Line Railway. (Courtesy of Guy Dunscomb)

HIGH NUMBER of this ten-wheeler is a leftover from previous owner. Old 949 ran on the Waterville Railway, a 5-mile Washington wheat hauler. (Courtesy of E. C. Towler)

CONSOLIDATION TYPE, or 2-8-0 wheel arrangement, was commonplace style of freight hauler known as "hogs" by railroaders. This one is No. 24 of the Idaho & Washington Northern.

TYPICAL YARD GOAT around turn of the century was the Northern Pacific Terminal Company's No. 3, an 0-6-0 switch engine. Pictured here with the hand-fired coal burner is Engineer J. Crader and Fireman Park Nugent; photo was taken in November, 1909.

SEATTLE CITY LIGHT, this is the 6-Spot of the short-line Skagit River Railway, backed by a transmission line tower of the power company the road served. (Courtesy of Guy L. Dunscomb)

MILWAUKEE ROAD FREIGHT DRAG crosses Hanson's Creek Bridge in the Cascade Mts. of Washington, hauled by two big electric motors. This line pierces Cascade Range via the Snoqualmie Tunnel. (Courtesy of The Milwaukee Road)

knocked out the ends, and lashed it into place for a substitute stack, much to the discomfiture of the Good Templars.

A grand celebration was held at Blaine on February 14, 1891, to celebrate the joining of the Fairhaven & Southern and the New Westminster & Southern. The trains from north and south arrived in Blaine almost simultaneously and the last spike ceremonies took place shortly after 10:45 A.M.

The entire program was carried off in elegant style, with no incidents to mar the amicable union of the two countries.

Not quite so peaceful was the meeting of the rails in Sedro-Woolley, where the lines of the Fairhaven & Southern, Seattle Northern, and the Seattle, Lake Shore & Eastern are intersected, forming a small 100-foot triangle. Construction crews of the Seattle Northern under Chief Engineer J. J. Cryderman clashed with the Lake Shore track gang when they met at the crossing site. A brisk free-for-all enlivened the meeting until cooler heads prevailed and the differences were ironed out by legal methods.

Another short line in the Bellingham area was the Bellingham Bay & Eastern Railroad. Built primarily as a coal hauler to serve the Blue Canyon mine near Lake Whatcom, the road engaged in a pitched battle with the Great Northern crews who attempted to prevent the erection of an overhead crossing of their line. The Bellingham Bay & Eastern was later acquired by Larson, Bloedel & Donovan for a logging road, and was extended to Wickersham in 1902. In 1903, the line was sold to the Northern Pacific.

JOHNNY COME LATELY

The last of the transcontinentals to breach the Rockies and cross the Pacific Northwest was the Milwaukee Road. The line had its inception in 1863 as the Milwaukee & St. Paul Railway and in 1874 the name was changed to the Chicago, Milwaukee & St. Paul Railway.

On November 28, 1905, the directors authorized construction of an extension from the end of track at Evarts, South Dakota, to the Pacific Ocean. Survey crews explored the western ranges for a feasible route for the new line, which was to be about 1,400 miles in length. The Northern Pacific and the Great Northern frowned upon the invasion of their domain and the Hill interests blocked the Columbia Gorge with the North Bank Road, the Portland & Seattle.

In March, 1906, the intruder filed for a right of way through the Snoqualmie Pass in Washington, and before long actual construction was under way.

The new road, known on the Pacific end as the Chicago, Milwaukee & Puget Sound, thrust into historic territory; the steel passed through Miles City, Forsyth, and Roundup, threading up the Musselshell to Harlowton and over the Belt Mountains west of Two Dot. Soon the whistling of Milwaukee engines was echoing across the path of the Lewis and Clark expedition, the tracks passing near a campsite at Three Forks, junction of the Madison and Jefferson

NORTHWEST PASSAGE. Engines 2509 and 3018 doublehead the "OLYMPIAN" of the Milwaukee Road in this 1912 photo taken at Hull Creek bridge near Garcia, Washington, before electrification through the Cascades. (Courtesy of the Milwaukee Road)

FREIGHT TRAIN AHOY. A tug churns up Puget Sound with a car float loaded with a cut of cars in the marine operations of the Milwaukee Road. (Courtesy of The Milwaukee Road)

rivers with the Missouri. Crossing the summit of the Rockies near Butte, the road dipped down to Missoula and then climbed the steep slopes of the Bitter Root Range.

At an elevation of 4,170 feet, the tracks pierced the summit of the Bitter Roots through a tunnel in St. Paul Pass and wound down into the St. Joe Valley of Idaho. The cost of the heavy rock work and grading made the Milwaukee the most expensive transcontinental built, averaging $55,000 per mile.

In one eight-mile section over twenty miles of track were laid to carry the road through the Bitter Roots, and this segment included a four-mile loop and eleven tunnels, plus several trestles and bridges.

The tunnel through St. Paul Pass, nearly two miles long, was bored through by gangs working from each end; when the two crews met in the middle of the 9,000-foot "rat hole," the headings were only 1/100ths of an inch out of

alignment. Most of the rock work was done by Swedish workmen.

At St. Joe, Idaho, a commissary and supply depot was established at the head of navigation for Grant, Henry & McFee, the railroad contractors. Construction camps were scattered through the region, and shanty towns blossomed near them. These mushroom villages consisted for the most part of saloons and gambling hells, eager to grab the ready cash of the gangs of laborers. Taft, at the east end of the big tunnel, was one of these wide-open boom towns.

Numerous accidents marred the construction records, one premature blast killing 5 men and injuring 20, many of them being badly mangled.

The great day for the Milwaukee Road came on March 18, 1909, when the Pacific Coast extension between Tacoma and Missoula was completed. The Chicago, Milwaukee & St. Paul and the Chicago, Milwaukee & Puget Sound were formally merged in 1913 as the present Chicago, Milwaukee, St. Paul & Pacific.

The Milwaukee Road launched a program of electrification and soon powerful "juice jacks" were sparking along beneath a great catenary system. Beginning at Harlowton, the electric zone ran west for 440 miles to Avery, Idaho. On the western end, a second electric zone reached from Othello, Washington, into Tacoma and Seattle, covering a 216-mile stretch of track.

The heavy cost of construction of the Pacific

SLIDE VALVE CONSOLIDATION, Engine 486 bears the initials of the Chicago, Milwaukee & St. Paul. The road combined with the Chicago, Milwaukee & Puget Sound to form the Chicago, Milwaukee, St. Paul & Pacific. (Courtesy of the Milwaukee Road)

Coast Extension, along with the electrification expenses, created a serious drain on the Milwaukee's finances, and was instrumental in causing the road to pass into a long-lasting receivership.

During the expansion years, the Milwaukee obtained control of the old Bellingham Bay & British Columbia Railroad in 1911. This short line ran from Bellingham to Sumas, on the Canadian border, and on to Glacier, with a branch from Hampton to Lynden. Service connections with this detached segment of Milwaukee Road trackage is maintained by the Milwaukee's "navy," a barge service operated on Puget Sound. This barge line also serves the section of Milwaukee trackage on the northern tip of the Olympic Peninsula, including Port Ludlow, Port Townsend, Port Angeles, and Disque. Other branch lines in the Northwest operate between Spokane and Metaline Falls; Cedar Falls to Everett, Plummer Junction to Marengo, Warden to Marcellus, Othello to Moses Lake, and a line from Beverly Junction to the atomic center of Hanford. From Tacoma, Milwaukee trains fan out to serve Aberdeen, Hoquiam, Willapa, Raymond and other locations along the Pacific. During the first World War, the Milwaukee absorbed the old Tacoma & Eastern, a logging road that ran to Tanwax and Kapowsin, and now forms a part of the line

PRAIRIE TYPE ENGINE 2000, a hand-fired coal eater, was typical of power in use on the Milwaukee Road about the time construction began on the line's extension to the Pacific Coast. (Courtesy of the Milwaukee Road)

to Morton and Ashford, the latter station serving Mt. Rainier Park.

The train and engine crews of the Milwaukee Road played a heroic role in the big fire of 1910 that swept through the pine forests of Idaho and Montana. Fires had been smouldering fitfully all that summer in the Bitter Roots, but the big blow-up came on the 20th of August. Canyons that had been hazy with blue wood smoke since May suddenly blossomed with angry red tongues of flame, pushed on by a brisk wind. The numerous small fires were soon combining, and a roaring inferno blasted through the pines, creating a veritable hell on earth.

Milwaukee trains hurried through the mountains, gathering up the fleeing inhabitants. Railroaders with blistered hands and faces stuck to their posts, and brought out train loads of refugees in cars with scorched and charred sides. One train, trapped between two walls of fire,

MILWAUKEE ROAD ELECTRIC MOTOR rushes the "Olympian Hiawatha" through the timbered bridge of the Cascade Mountains in Washington. (Courtesy of the Milwaukee Road)

BELLINGHAM BAY & BRITISH COLUMBIA R.R. engine "D. O. MILLS" was built by H. J. Booth & Co., San Francisco, in 1868. Bearded engineer is Billy Mann. (Courtesy of Fred Jukes, Blaine, Wn.)

sought haven in a tunnel and safely weathered out the big burn, its cargo of human lives unharmed. The stations of Taft, Haugan, Tuscor, and DeBorgia were all hard hit. When the ashes cooled, 16 Milwaukee bridges, from 120 to 775 feet in length, were found to be in charred ruins. The survivors of the great fire of 1910 had ample reason to be grateful to the brave crews of the Milwaukee Road for their courageous efforts in the evacuation of refugees from the red hell.

RAILS TO YREKA

When the rails of the California & Oregon Railroad were being pushed north into the Siskiyous in 1886, the citizens of Yreka were cheered by the thought that trains would soon rumble into their village.

A committee of Yreka businessmen was dispatched to contact the officials of the parent Central Pacific to urge that the line of the new railroad pass through the city, but the hopes of the community were dashed when the reply came back. The main line was to pass up the

valley some 8 miles to the east and the toot of the engine whistles would be indeed faint in Yreka.

The townspeople met in the firehouse at Yreka in April of 1888, and when the meeting adjourned, the Yreka Branch Railroad Company was born.

Contract for construction was let to the firm of Gillis & McMahan and the rocky slopes of Siskiyou County soon echoed the noise of railroad building. By the time autumn of 1889 was cooling the foothills, the line was completed and placed in operation.

The standard gauge tracks crossed Yreka Creek, then climbed the barren flank of Butcher Hill, passing the old Chinese cemetery, and dropped on down to a connection with the California & Oregon Railroad (now Southern Pacific) at Montague. The little road was about 8 miles long, and the steepest grade was slightly over 2%, this being on Butcher Hill.

Since cash was in such short supply, the Yreka Railroad rented a locomotive from the Central Pacific and used it until the Baldwin Locomotive Works delivered old Number 1. The

One-spot was built in 1889, and was a 2-4-2 tank type, burning wood.

The road suffered considerable flood damage in the winter of 1889-90, the grade on the east bank of Yreka Creek washing away. The road was restored under the able management of Tom Schultz, and soon was again making a profit for the owners. Mr. Schultz died in 1898 and the position of general manager passed to Mr. Harry L. Walther, an experienced railroad man.

The short line continued to prosper and another locomotive was acquired in 1898. This engine, numbered "2," was purchased second-hand from the old Hogg road up in Oregon, where she had been the Oregon Pacific's No. 11. She was built by the Cooke Works in 1886, and was a 4-4-0 type.

No accurate record has been found regarding the disposition of the Yreka's No. 1, but she was reportedly sold to one of the numerous logging railroads in the state of Washington.

In 1905, the small fry of Yreka were delighted to learn that a circus was coming to town. After a grand performance, the cars of the circus train were coupled together and the hogger widened on the latch for a run at the Butcher Hill grade. Shortly after leaving the Yreka depot and crossing the creek, the rails spread and several cars of the circus special were toppled over. One of the cars was loaded with some of the wild animals belonging to the troupe, and when the dust settled, the railroad was $2,500 out of pocket for damages.

About this time, the Yreka Railroad was purchased by Mr. Alex. J. Rosborough, and

early in 1906 the local papers were jubilant over the fact that Rosborough had acquired capital to complete the extension from Yreka to Scott Valley.

The blow fell on April 18th, with news of the terrible earthquake and fire that had hit San Francisco. The financial firm backing the extension had suffered great losses in the disaster and the extension project died before a single spade of earth had been turned.

Hard times beset the little road, and in 1920 it seemed doomed to be abandoned, but the business men of Yreka again took it over. In 1928 the line was sold to H. A. De Vaux, representing the Klamath River Holding Company, and the name was changed to the Yreka Western Railroad Corporation.

The railroad passed through the hands of several other owners, including H. T. Kellogg and C. W. Faucett, and in 1935 went into receivership. The receiver for the road was Mr. Orlo G. Steele, who still resides in Yreka, although now retired. When Mr. Steele took charge of the road, it was in almost derelict condition. The earnings of the road were spent in repairing the track and equipment, and two locomotives were acquired from the State Belt Line of San Francisco. These engines were numbered 7 and 8, and came to the Yreka Western in 1944.

The receivership was terminated on October 1, 1948, the new owner of the road being the late A. D. Schader. Steele was retained as vice-president and operating officer.

At present, the manager is Mr. Lynn T.

FIRST PASSENGER TRAIN over Siskiyous, California to Oregon, pulled by this engine and crew Dec. 17, 1887. L. to r. Cond. George Morgan, Eng. Jack Clark, unknown, work train foreman Jack O'Neill, three unknown, asst. foreman Gus Loew, others unknown. (Courtesy Sisk. Co. Hist. Soc.)

Cecil, a genial, handsome young railroad executive.

The Yreka Western is still an all-steam road, but Mr. Cecil believes a Diesel will soon replace the two Mikado type oil-burners now owned, both purchased from the McCloud River Railroad. No. 19, still retaining her McCloud River number, bears a builder's plate indicating that she was Baldwin's 42,000th locomotive, outshopped in 1915. She reportedly came to the McCloud River line from a Mexican mining company, and is said to have played a part in Pancho Villa's border campaigns. The Yreka Western acquired her in 1953.

Other locomotives have chuffed over the short line before passing on into oblivion. Oldest of these was No. 3, a little 10-wheeler built by Schenectady in 1882 as the No. 48 of the Southern Pacific of New Mexico coming to Yreka in 1906.

The 9 and 10 were both Prairie types bought second-hand from the McCloud River R.R.; No. 10 was scrapped but No. 9 passed on to the Amador Central and then up to the Nezperce Railroad in Idaho. The newest engine the Yreka Western owned in recent years was a 2-8-2 numbered 100. Built by Brooks in 1920, she originally ran on the Portland, Astoria & Pacific, later being owned by the Long-Bell Lbr. Co. and was sold to a scrap metal concern by the Yreka line in 1955.

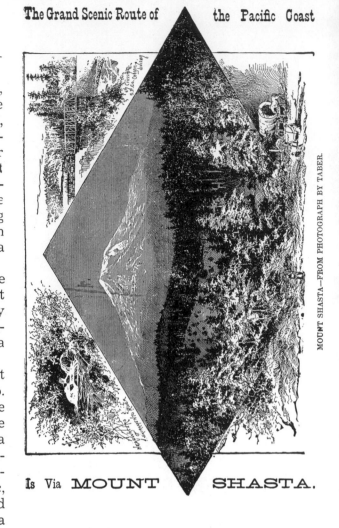

MOUNT SHASTA—FROM PHOTOGRAPH BY TABER.

Is Via MOUNT SHASTA.

TEA FOR TWO. This duet of wood-burners doublehead a tea train over Sierras. Shipments of tea and raw silk from Orient were given priority rights to East Coast. This photo made on Central Pacific; both Northern Pacific and Great Northern vied for lucrative trade from Puget Sound ports. (Courtesy of Southern Pacific)

WESTERN CLASSIC. Rim rock frames an early Central Pacific train in the Palisade Canyon of Nevada. Engine appears to be No. 152, the "WHITE FOX." (Courtesy of Southern Pacific)

WHEELS IN ACTION. Five Southern Pacific engines boost a freight drag up a stiff climb in the Siskiyou Mountains.

A gas "skunk" carried passengers for a time, but the road finally abandoned all passenger service and today it operates strictly as a freight hauler. The present generation has nearly forgotten the old-timers of the Yreka. Engineer E. F. Dean, who pulled the throttle on "Old Betsy," has long since passed away. Also gone from the pike are Engineers Archie De Lamontonia and Charlie Lewis, along with Fireman Jack Frizell.

If Diesel power comes, it will be a sad day when the smoky iron horses no longer labor up Butcher Hill or pound across the Shasta River bridge toward Montague.

The growl of internal combustion engines can never replace the thunder of blasting steam exhaust, and the blat of Diesel air horns will disturb the ghosts of the old Chinese miners slumbering away Eternity atop the barren ridge, where they have been lulled these many years by the mellow chime of steam whistles.

BEHIND SIX HORSES ROLLS "CALISTOGA," just completed at Vulcan Iron Works, San Francisco, in May, 1867; built for Napa Valley R.R., later Vaca Valley R.R.'s "VACAVILLE," she became Vaca Valley & Clear Lake's 1-Spot, thence to Central Pacific and later to Union Coal Co. (Courtesy of Southern Pacific)

"WHITE EAGLE" was the name assigned Central Pacific's No. 116. Early engines bore a wide variety of names, including birds, animals, rivers, prominent personages, mythological characters, etc. One series on C.P. included "DRIVER," "CLIPPER," "RACER," "RATTLER," "RANGER," "ROVER," and "RUNNER." (Courtesy of Southern Pacific)

McCLOUD RIVER RAILROAD combination coaches, pulled by No. 11, handled U.S. mail, Wells Fargo & Co. express on northern California run.

NEVADA-CALIFORNIA-OREGON RAILWAY was a 3-foot gauge line that ran from Reno, Nevada, to Lakeview, Oregon. It was begun as a private road by Moran Bros. of New York, and later became part of the Southern Pacific Lines and standard gauged.

EARLY-DAY PIGGY-BACK, showing how narrow gauge locomotives were hauled over standard gauge lines. The ornate little Mogul was built by Brooks in 1873 as No. 2, the "KATE CONNOR," for the Salt Lake, Sevier Valley & Pioche Railroad; road was unable to pay for engine and it was taken over by Eureka & Palisade, a Nevada short line, where it was renamed "EUREKA." Note the elaborate painting on tender and cab panels, ornamental brass eagle on top of sand dome.

KLAMATH NORTHERN RAILWAY boasted No. 204, the "D. E. GARNER," one of few remaining named locomotives in the country; engine was painted a gaudy red with white and aluminum trim, ran from mill at Gilchrist to junction with Southern Pacific. Espee firemen Dick Metzger and Del Green stand by cylinder.

HUGE FUNNEL STACK and oil headlight dominate this Mogul built by the Brooks Locomotive Works as No. 87 of the Utah Northern. Narrow-gauge line was started by Mormon Church in 1871, later purchased by Union Pacific and absorbed into the Oregon Short Line. Photo was taken at Dillon, Utah, in 1884.

CALIFORNIA LUMBER HAULER, this is old No. 1 of the McCloud River Railroad, a 98-mile short line in the Siskiyou County pinelands. She was built by Baldwin in 1891 and was originally California Ry. No. 2; McCloud River later renumbered her 12, scrapped her in 1932.

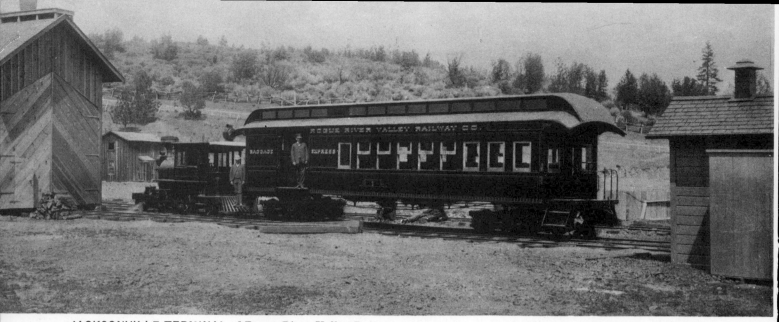

JACKSONVILLE TERMINAL of Rogue River Valley Railway. Big coach towers over tiny 2-4-2 type steamer. Road ran about 7 miles to connect with Oregon & California R.R. at Medford when the O & C by-passed the historic old mining town. Loss of main line cost Jacksonville the county seat. (From a Britt glass plate, Oregon Collection, Univ of Ore.)

STIFF CLIMB! Whitney Co. Climax 801, named "MOLLY-O," gets a helping hand from a cable while mounting a nearly-perpendicular track on a logging incline in western Oregon.

CITY SLICKER. This Forney type locomotive was far from her native haunts when she posed for this picture as the Rogue River Valley Railway Company's No. 5. She was originally used on the famous elevated street railways in New York City, then saw service on the Barnum family's short line connecting Jacksonville and Medford, Oregon, in the heart of the Rogue River Valley. (Courtesy of M. Dale Newton)

Call The Big Hook

RAIL THRILLS

In the rough and ready days of railroading, accidents were frequent and accepted as a necessary evil. In the Northwest, tracks were new and often hastily laid through rough terrain and nature occasionally interfered with rail operations. Primitive cars and engines were subject to mechanical failure and the working conditions of the crews contributed to the growing list of accidents.

One of the first recorded accidents in the Pacific Northwest occurred on the Oregon & California Railroad on September 12, 1870. The original Oregon Central tracks between East Portland and Car Shops (now Brooklyn) were being relocated away from the banks of the Willamette River and crossed over swampy ground on a timber trestle. On the first run over this new line, the trestling sank beneath the weight of the train and plunged the loco-

motive "PORTLAND," a baggage car, and a flat car down twenty feet to the ground below. Three of the crew were injured.

Although this was the first known instance of bridge collapses in the Northwest, it was by no means the last. One of the more spectacular bridge mishaps occurred in August, 1894, on the Oregon Railway & Navigation Company line near Alto, Washington. A freight train started down the steep grade toward McKay's Hollow, spanned by Bridge 321. This timber structure was about 850 feet long and 97 feet high. As his engine neared the far side of the curved trestle, Engineer J. M. Jessee glanced down and saw that the timbers were falling beneath his locomotive. Instinctively, he yanked the throttle wide open and the engine leaped forward, breaking loose from the train.

The locomotive reached the fill at the end of the bridge in safety, but the rails were jerked

BIG HOOKS AT WORK. Two steam wrecking cranes up-right a locomotive that plunged over an embankment near Oakland, Oregon; engineer was killed in accident. Equipment is on a spur laid to reach wreckage, as engine came to rest where fallen tree shows at left. (Harry Barrell photo, courtesy of Fred Chapman)

TRAGIC REMINDER of dangers of "bucking" snow, this picture shows how engines piled up when one derailed; cab of one turned over shows at left, others are jackknifed in tangled mess that proved fatal to an engineer.

out from under its wheels, leaving the engine standing on the bare ties.

Brakemen David Wright and Fred Harrison had finished turning up their retaining valves and were seated on top of the freight cars near the center of the train when the bridge fell, while Conductor Watson was in the caboose. None of them were seriously injured, although all three were hospitalized.

In the early days, before improved brakes were applied to rolling stock, the roads of the Northwest were the scenes of frequent runaways. Some of these came to a tragic end, such as the O.R. & N. wreck at the foot of Meeker Hill in the Snake River Valley. Engineer Van Dresser and Conductor McDonald were in charge of an extra freight consisting of 17 loads of wheat on the night of November 20th, 1890. When they started down the steep hill, the number of retainers proved insufficient. Van Dresser whistled for brakes and the two trainmen, Loechler and Cameron, ran from

car to car, winding on the brake wheels. Conductor McDonald cut off the caboose, sensing that the train was doomed. For seven miles the train rocketed through the black night, gaining momentum, while Van Dresser stuck at his post in the cab, fighting to regain control by using sand and reversing his engine, while the brakemen futilely swung their weight on the hand brakes. Finally the speed became too great and the train literally flew off the tracks and piled down a bank. Fireman Wilson was crushed when the engine rolled over him and Brakeman Loechler was dead in the wreckage, badly broken. Engineer Van Dresser and Brakeman Cameron miraculously escaped with only minor injuries.

The torrential rains that doused the raw grades in the region often set the stage for accidents. One such wreck happened in the early 1900's on the Esquimalt & Nanaimo Railroad on Vancouver Island. Rounding a curve on Malahat Mountain during a heavy downpour,

174

IN THE DRINK. Consolidation type freight locomotive took a header into river near Pendleton in early 1900's; second engine involved in wreck is inspected by spectators on bank in right background. (Oregon Collection, University of Oregon)

a freight engine struck a large boulder loosened by the rains and left the rails. The locomotive broke loose from the tender and plunged 150 feet down the hill, killing the head brakeman. The engineer was thrown clear and the fireman escaped with minor injuries.

Along the coastal slopes of the Cascades, the thick fogs that often blanketed the valleys slowed rail traffic and made life miserable for the operating crews. Poor visibility and signals obscured by the wooly shroud caused a number of mishaps.

Even the narrow-gauge White Pass & Yukon had its share of accidents. One of these involved Engine 66, being used in helper service from Skagway to White Pass Summit. Two helper engines had been used to boost a freight up one rainy night in 1905, and were returning "light" to Skagway. Engine 66, with "Rotary Bill" Simpson at the throttle, was in the lead as the two helpers drifted back down the steep

grade. At the former location of Bridge 17 D, a new fill had been constructed and through the rain-drenched night Simpson saw that the rails across it appeared to be sagging. He big-holed his brake valve, yanked a warning blast on the whistle, and then he and Fireman Moriarity jumped to safety. Engine 66 broke away from the other locomotive and came to rest on her back 100 feet down the mountainside.

The advent of block signals, protective devices, improved track and equipment, and better working conditions greatly improved the safety records of the railroads, and today there is no safer means of public transport than the flanged wheel on the steel rail. Occasionally the Gods of the High Iron frown on man's puny efforts and a pile-up occurs, but the wild old days of frequent collisions and disastrous wrecks are only an unpleasant memory.

SALVAGE OPERATION. While crew of laborers remove sacks of grain and stave bolts from wreckage of Oregon Pacific train that fell into Yaquina River, an engine and box car are eased cautiously out onto remaining portion of trestle to rescue locomotive from its precarious perch. Cab roof of engine was nearly torn off when span collapsed, but Engineer Casteel and fireman escaped with only minor injuries. (Courtesy Oregon Historical Society)

HEAVY RAINS CAUSED MUD SLIDE in Pass Creek Canyon that blocked main stem of Southern Pacific about 1907. Slide was struck by passenger train, sending both road engine and helper tumbling into deep ravine; engineer on helper locomotive, Wm. Weichlein, was killed here. The "hook" drags Rhode Island Loco. Works' engine up to main line.

FATAL PRANK. Three farm hands, unloaded by an Oregon & California trainman, sought revenge and tried to line stub switch at Albany Junction to send a main line passenger train up the Lebanon Branch. The train, drawn by Engine 23, struck the open switch and piled up, fatally injuring Engr. "Big Jack" Miller and Fireman Quin Guthrie. The date of the wreck was August 28, 1889. One of the men responsible was sent to Oregon penitentiary. (Courtesy of Southern Pacific)

DRIFTING SAND blown by "gentle zephyrs" along Columbia River caused this double-header to pile up on O.R.&N. east of The Dalles about 1890. "Blow sand" was a constant source of trouble along this section. (Courtesy of Union Pacific R.R.)

STRAYING COW UPSET THE 4-SPOT of the old Oregon & California Railroad somewhere on West Side line in 1880's. Relief engine at left shows the three-slot rear drawbar for coupling to cars of varying heights. (Courtesy of R. M. Bodley)

END OF THE LINE. Carlton Consolidated Lbr. Co. No. 70, a Lima Shay, ran away on the high line above Tillamook Gate. Formerly owned by Twin Falls Logging Co. of Yacolt, Wn., she was sold for junk to Clyde Equipment Co. of Portland. (Photo by courtesy of Ben Griffiths)

"OFF AGIN, ON AGIN" as in the episode between Finnegan and Flannigan, derailments on pikes in the Northwest were frequent in the early days. New track, laid in haste and poorly maintained, was often the cause of these mishaps which usually caused more delay than damage. Object under boot of man in foreground is a metal "frog" used for re-railing cars.

STOCK TRAIN CRASH. Wreck on the Portland Division in the 1890's killed a number of sheep, one of which shows at left. Engine was S.P. 1765, built in the Sacramento Shops in 1888 as the Central Pacific's No. 238, later became S.P. 2194. The big wood-burner was equipped with Master Mechanic A. J. Stevens' patent valve gear, called the "monkey motion" by S.P. enginemen.

DISPUTED PASSAGE. Engines 295 and 240 of the Northern Pacific locked horns in this head-on collision in Eastern Washington on May 17, 1909. The accident occurred near Ellensburg (Pautzke photo)

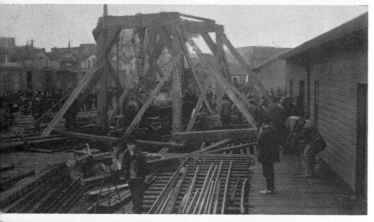

INTERIOR VIEW OF COACH that fell with the Lake Labish trestle in 1890. Photo shows gas lamps, wooden window shutters, and (at far right end) the stove that heated early-day passenger cars.

DRASTIC EFFECT OF BOILER EXPLOSION is shown by this photo taken in 1912. Southern Pacific Engine 2538 was helping a freight up Rice Hill when her crown sheet let go, killing the engineer and fireman. Boiler was tossed high into air and landed several car-lengths away from its frame and wheels. (Courtesy of Herbert F. Ogden)

PHOTOGRAPHERS HAD A FIELD DAY around turn of the century when Oregon & California Railroad's Engine 1250 dropped through dock at Jefferson Street station in Portland, landing in shallow water of Willamette River. Engine was fished out by means of scaffold and block and tackle, using manila rope, pulled by other locomotives.

RAILROADER'S NIGHTMARE, THE HEAD-ON COLLISION. One engineer rode to his death and several crewmen were injured in this wreck, caused by a crew overlooking a train order. Smash took place on Portland Division of S.P. in May, 1918. (Courtesy of C. L. McGrew)

"LEAP FROG" ON THE "BILLY GOAT." Belpaire-boilered Mogul tried to climb over Engine No. 450 in this collision on the Great Northern near Tampico, Montana, on July 4th, 1899. Engine was so securely loaded on 450's ruined tender that both locomotives were towed away to shops in this position.

NOT ON THE TIME-CARD! Head-on collision occurred at Gold Hill, Oregon, in early 1900's when engineer on the 2191, at left, lost control of his train and crashed into the 2141, standing on the Southern Pacific main line at the Gold Hill tank. Both crews jumped clear. (Courtesy of Floyd Eddings)

LATE FOR DINNER! No. 1 of the Salem, Falls City & Western Ry. has climbed the rails and hit the ties near the end of a short trestle. Road ran out of Dallas, Oregon, and was built by Louis and Geo. T. Gerlinger and L. Gerlinger, Jr. (Courtesy of F. A. Bewley)

The Loggers

HANDWRITING ON THE WALL. The advent of steam locomotives, such as this homemade wood burner, marked a revolution in Northwest logging that was to drive the bull teams into oblivion. The crude logging train, skid road, and four yoke of "hay burners" were operated in the Coos Bay region. (Courtesy of Ross Youngblood)

BROAD GAUGE was feature of Gualala River Ry. Engines 2, 4, and 3, shown here, were built to fit 5-foot, 8½-inch track originally used by logging cars pulled by teams of horses on California road.

TOOTH PICKS AT TIDEWATER. Little Shay of the Simpson Lumber Company backs out to dumping grounds with logs loaded on sets of disconnected trucks, or "bunks." Operation was at Tarheel, on Coos Bay below present port of Empire. (Kinsey photo, courtesy of Ross Youngblood)

TRIM LOG HAULER. The wood-burner pictured here is Booth-Kelly's logging engine No. 1, a neat 2-6-2 type. (Courtesy of L. Sinnar)

BRAKIES WORE CAULKS on the logging roads of the Northwest. This photo of the Blazier Logging Co. operations was taken near Cape Horn, Washington, in 1912. Engine No. 1, a Heisler gear-driven model, was lettered "Washington Northern R.R. Co." (Courtesy Oregon Historical Society)

SORENSEN LOGGING CO.'S 3-SPOT, a Climax geared engine, hauls 5 logs cut from a single tree in the region along lower Columbia River. (E. A. Coe photo, courtesy O. V. Matthews)

TYPICAL SHAY is this two-truck wood-burner, operated by Leona Mills Lbr. Co. near Drain, Oregon. (Courtesy of Walter J. Bryan)

SADDLE-TANKER No. 9, operated by the Flora Logging Company, helped denude Oregon's Coast Range. Logging road connected with Carlton & Coast R.R.; engine built by Vulcan Iron Works, Wilkes-Barre, Pennsylvania. (Angelus Studio Photo)

CARLTON & COAST RAILROAD operated rod engines such as No. 11 from Carlton to Fairdale, Oregon, where Shays took over for the climb up a steep switchback to logging camps in the Coast Range. Logs were dumped into Carlton Lake, formed by damming up North Fork of Yamhill River, for storage before being fed to hungry saws of Carlton mill. (Tecrasilk Photo)

ARCATA & MAD RIVER RAILROAD'S ENGINE No. 6, hauling redwood timber north of Humboldt Bay. Road was built in 1883 to unusual gauge of three feet, nine and one-half inches. (Courtesy of Carl Christensen)

OLD SLOW & EASY. The Oregon & South Eastern built east from Cottage Grove to the Bohemia mining district in early 1900's. Engine 3 was formerly used on the historic Virginia & Truckee. O. & S. E. later became Oregon Pacific & Eastern. (Angelus Studio photo)

"BIG JACK" was the name assigned to Eng. 2501 of the Whitney Company. Rod engine was used on their logging railroad; they had extensive operations in Tillamook County, Oregon.

ANATOLE MALLET, a Frenchman, is credited with the original design of this type of locomotive and railroaders still call engines of this style "Malleys." Although usually associated with larger lines in mountainous terrain, this Mallet compound was used on the logging road of the Weyerhaeuser Timber Company.

COMMON CARRIER. Mikado, or "Mike" type No. 17 bears the lettering of the Portland & Southwestern R.R. Co., the common carrier portion of a lower Columbia River logging line.

OREGON, CALIFORNIA & EASTERN RAILROAD winds east from Klamath Falls to Bly, is operated alternately by Great Northern and Southern Pacific. Engine 2 of the O. C. & E. was built by Baldwin in 1888 for the Buffalo, Rochester & Pittsburgh R.R. and was later Spokane International's No. 12 before coming to the 65-mile pike operating into the Sprague River region. (Courtesy of Guy L. Dunscomb)

THE LOGGERS

No story of Northwest railroading would be complete without a tribute to the logging lines of the region, and a salute to the rugged men who operated them.

The main line men, accustomed to fast track, good equipment, and orderly operation, looked down their noses at their brothers "in the brush," but the saga of the logging lines is woven with colorful threads of valor and courage. The ribbons of steel did not begin to thrust into the timber in any quantity until about 1890. Steam donkeys came, forcing the plodding bull teams off the skid roads, and soon the bark of the locomotive was heard in the "tall and uncut."

By the turn of the century, logging railroading was firmly established in the evergreen empire on the North Pacific, and the lines reached the peak of their climb between the First World War and the mid-1920's. When the demand for logs boomed, any "gyppo" logger who could mortgage his soul for enough cash to buy a geared "lokey" and a few miles

of worn-out rail could go into the logging railroad game. Spindly piling trestles crept across yawning canyons, and the rusty iron threaded over the highest ridges. The use of the Climax, Heisler, and Shay types of geared engines made grades feasible that would have seemed impossible to main line crews. Over these jerry-built pikes, around torturous curves, and across quaking bridges the logging crews nursed their trains. Most of these short lines hauled their logs on railway trucks, more commonly called "bunks." The logs themselves formed the connections between these 4-wheeled trucks and it took a smooth hand on the throttle to bring out such a string of loads. The type of equipment usually prevented the use of air brakes and some of the cattiest "car hands" in the world were the caulk-shod brakies who dropped these trains down the hill with hand brakes; leaping from car to car, clubbing brakes with their iron "hickeys," theirs was a job that took sheer guts. The logging pikes used the man-killing link and pin couplers long after such devices had been outlawed on other railroads. Derailments on these pikes were almost daily

WEST COAST BOOMER. This Schenectady 10-wheeler was built in 1882 as the No. 45 of the Southern Pacific of New Mexico. She later became Southern Pacific's 204, then 1678, and was finally assigned the number 2090. In 1907 she was sold to the Coos Bay, Roseburg & Eastern Railroad & Navigation Company and numbered 4, as shown here. When the Southern Pacific absorbed the latter road in 1915, the old 4-6-0 returned to the fold and was given back her previous number, 2090. She was scrapped in 1918. (Courtesy of Guy L. Dunscomb)

occurences and logging railroaders were experts in the use of frogs, jacks, blocks and tackle. Runaways were frequent and often fatal. The wise crew unloaded when a cut of loaded cars got out of control on a 4 or 5 per cent grade, for it was considered better to walk back to camp than to be dug out piecemeal from under a smashed locomotive and a jumble of huge logs and car wheels.

Not all logging roads remained in crude condition. Major lines such as the Long-Bell Company, Simpson, Weyerhaeuser, and other operators ran logging lines that equalled or bettered some short line common carriers. In the pine country, the neat power of the Hines Lumber Co. and of Brooks-Scanlon was a delight to the eye. Whole camps of buildings constructed on flat cars were moved along the track as the loggers cut deeper into the vast stands of virgin timber.

From an operating standpoint, no condition was too tough for the logging road crews. A small logging company in Oregon had a stand of timber west of Willamina that they desired to haul to a stream where the logs could be floated out to a sawmill. They bought a donkey and a Shay locomotive and set out across country, since no rail line extended into their domain. The donkey would yard itself ahead, anchor, then drag the old Shay, which was mounted on a log sled, up to it. Over and over, this procedure was repeated. Once or twice the Shay rolled over, but was soon righted, slightly the worse for her tumble. At length the goal was reached and soon logs were rolling behind her.

In the heyday of steam in the timber, logging railroads flourished from British Columbia to the heart of the California redwoods. The coming of the motor truck and Diesel "cat" has now largely supplanted the colorful logging railway, and only a few operations continue hauling their logs by train.

Climb a random ridge in the coastal mountains and stroll through the fireweed and young alders. Soon you will stumble over an old tie or a rusty cable buried in the fern. Follow the brushy grade and you will come upon a skeleton of a trestle, charred by fire or bleached by sun and rain. Mark it well, for it is a monument to a sturdy breed, the logging railroader.

NECESSITY WAS THE MOTHER OF INVENTION in Coos County. Local citizenry built this home-made locomotive to run on wooden rails, using a vertical boiler and gear drive. Earlier Isthmus Transit portage road had used a mule to pull flatcar over similar track. (Courtesy of Jack's Photo Shop)

HIGH-STEPPING No. 2 was the pride of Coos Bay, Roseburg & Eastern R.R. & Nav. Co. and was built by Cuyahoga Locomotive Works in 1872. Engine was brought to Coos County in 1893. Brakeman Ralph Lane holds bell cord, Fireman Billy Cox kneels on running board, boy seated between them is Ben Chandler, now a retired Coos Bay banker and son of C. B. R. & E. Supt. Wm. Chandler. Engineer holding oil can is John Herron while Conductor Bill Denning stands below Benny Chandler. Brakeman holding flag is unidentified. Engine was decorated for a baseball excursion. (Courtesy of Robt. H. Wilson)

AT THE BEAVER HILL MINE, a string of empty gondolas is spotted for coal loading by Coos Bay, Roseburg & Eastern's Engine No. 5. The coal went by rail to Marshfield, where it was loaded on vessels for ocean trip to San Francisco. Odd caboose behind engine had platforms at each end large enough to carry tools and small shipments of way freight.

GOOD-BYE, BULLS! Primitive "lokeys" such as this one, reputed to be the first in Coos County, soon drove the colorful bull teams out of the Northwest timber. Rails that replaced the old skid roads are now nearly extinct, having given way to fleets of logging trucks, and the Shays that blasted up through the "tall and uncut" are museum pieces; only the older generations of timber beasts recall the rides between camp and the woods behind the snorting old "side-winders." (Courtesy of Jack Slattery, Jack's Photo Service, Coos Bay)

RAILROADING AT SEA LEVEL, this Coos Bay, Roseburg & Eastern R.R. & Navigation Co. locomotive shunts a mixed train on the docks at Marshfield (now Coos Bay) Oregon. Schooners, both sail and steam, lie alongside to discharge cargo and load lumber. Trestle in rear led up to bunkers where railroad loaded coal into sea-going vessels. (Courtesy of J. Slattery, Jack's Photo Service, Coos Bay)

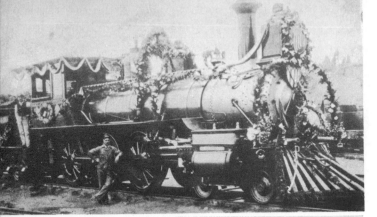

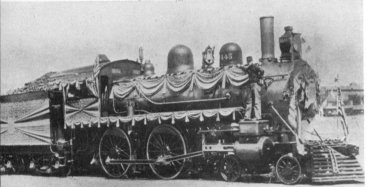

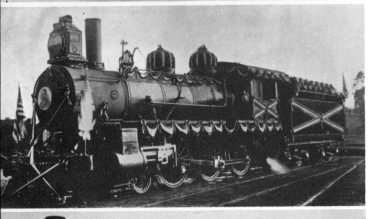

All Dolled Up

Decorating engines for special occasions was a frequent practice in by-gone years, with some extremely colorful results.

Flags and greenery ornament Southern Pacific's 115. Note eagle figure on top of sand dome, porrait of Lincoln on front of smokebox.

Cannon, sabers, muskets, and drum nestle amid flowers on this 4-6-0 built in the Central Pacific's Sacramento shops.

Bunting, flags, and shield set off Southern Pacific's 1445, built in 1900 by the Cooke works.

Southern Pacific's 2239 also handled Pres. Teddy Roosevelt in 1903.

Southern Pacific's No. 2251 is shown with the first train to enter Klamath Falls, Oregon. (Courtesy of Southern Pacific)

Astoria & Columbia River No. 8, leased to S.P., hauled Teddy Roosevelt to Berkeley in 1903. Left to right, Dan Kellogg, Asst. Master Mechanic; Bob Aiken, Engineer; Jack Muir; Harry Stevenson, Traveling Engineer; Fireman Frank Adamson in cab window, Traveling Fireman Fred Sugden in gangway. (Courtesy of D. J. Welch)

Oddities

Southern Pacific's 2244 decorated for a Presidential Special.

Thin blue line of G.A.R. vets decorate train of Rogue River Valley R.R., hauled behind quaint little Engine No. 1 at Medford. (Courtesy of M. Dale Newton)

This was railroading? Steam locomotive No. 3, the "GOLTRA PARK," ran on Albany, Oregon, Street Railway; little engine was a genuine 0-4-2 type disguised under a coach body to fool skittish horses. Such engines were once common on interurban lines and were called the "Dummy" type. Bearded conductor had previously operated Car No. 1 as a horsecar on street railway, which served business district and ran to Southern Pacific and Oregon Pacific depots.

Mountain climber. Southern Pacific's cab-in-front No. 4200 was built by Baldwin in 1939. With her 63 inch drivers and 250 pounds of steam pressure on her gauge, she and her sisters boosted drags and "varnish" over mountain grades to the tune of roaring exhausts and the pounding of 16 driving wheels. (Courtesy of G. M. Best)

Wind splitter! Sharp-pointed nose distinguished this McKeen gas coach that was Motor Car 1 of the Salem, Falls City & Western. Auto at left is forerunner of hordes that killed branch line passenger trains. (Angelus Studio Photograph)

Steam Of All Ages

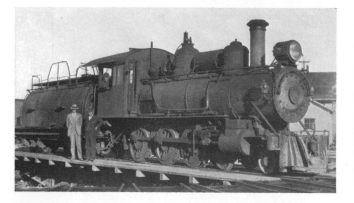

NORTHWESTERN PACIFIC'S 1st No. 3 was a Baldwin 4-4-0 built in 1884. She was formerly the Eel River & Eureka No. 2 and bore the name, "EUREKA." The little wood-burner was retired in 1916. (Courtesy of Southern Pacific)

COLT WITH A CAPPED STACK. 10-wheeler No. 5 of the Nevada-California-Oregon Railroad, a narrow-gauge Baldwin, is shown in 1927, when the line was being converted to standard gauge. (Courtesy of Southern Pacific)

A PAIR OF OLD-TIMERS. Early auto and Northwestern Pacific's No. 13 were both right-hand drives. Photo was taken near Eureka, California, in 1911. The 13 was built by Baldwin in 1875 as the "COLORADO SPRINGS" of the Santa Fe, later becoming San Francisco & North Western No. 6 before coming to N.W.P., where she served until 1929. (Courtesy of Southern Pacific)

SLIMGAUGE FREIGHTER. Oregonian Railway's No. 6 shuffles cars at White's, junction with the Western Oregon Railroad. Built by Porter in 1880, she had 35½ inch drivers, 12x16 inch cylinders. She was sold to the Sierra Valleys in 1895.

A PAIR OF FIRSTS. Western Pacific Engine 104, upper, stands ready to leave Salt Lake City with the road's first passenger train on August 20, 1910. A day later, Engine 94 headed the same train across lofty Spanish Creek Trestle near Keddie, California. (Courtesy of Western Pacific Railroad)

Passing Parade

PASSING PARADE. A sampler of Northwest motive power from the noted Jukes Collection.

Canadian National's 371 at North Kamloops, B.C. Unusual feature was injector pipes delivering water through bell frame.

Great Northern's 457 was a Mogul built by Brooks in early '90's.

Northern Pacific's 14, a 4-8-0, was originally cross compound.

Northern Pacific 78 was one of many 2-8-0's built between 1887 and 1890.

Canadian Pacific's 5211 when in passenger service out of Penticton, B.C., in recent years.

Canadian Pacific's 5310 at North Bend, B.C., about 1942.

Canadian Pacific's 2705 in the twilight years of steam.   (All photos, courtesy of Fred Jukes)

AUTHOR'S PET ENGINE was Southern Pacific No. 2770, which he fired on mixed train on Tillamook Branch, the former P. R. & N. line. Photo shows old gal as yard engine in Eugene shortly before she was retired in 1956. (R. E. Dunsmoor photo, courtesy of C. J. Riedel)

So ends a century of Northwest railroading, a golden era
of steam and steel whose close can be told in one word,

DIESELIZED!